Beningbrough Hall

Lucy Peltz and Jacob Simon

National
Portrait
Gallery

'Possess'd with the Spirit of Building'

The man and the house

A wealthy orphan

In September 1704 the twenty-year-old John Bourchier arrived in Rome. He had already known tragedy and good fortune, having lost both his parents by the age of eleven and having inherited the prosperous Beningbrough estate at sixteen. Bourchier's fourteen months in Rome would change his life again.

A grand tourist

Seeing the historic sites of Italy was becoming an essential part of every young English gentleman's education. Many took it as an excuse for drunken misbehaviour, but Bourchier seems to have been a studious tourist. He was particularly fascinated by the great Baroque palaces and churches of the city. Such was his enthusiasm that he acquired a copy of Domenico de Rossi's newly published *Studio d'Architettura Civile*, which provided a lavishly illustrated guide to these buildings and a source of inspiration when Bourchier decided to rebuild his family home after his return to Yorkshire.

Yorkshire Baroque

The North Riding boasts some of the great country houses of the English Baroque. Pre-eminent is Castle Howard, which was designed by John Vanbrugh in 1699. Astonishingly, Vanbrugh was still an amateur architect when he built Castle Howard, and his achievement stimulated amateur architects among the local gentry to try their hand, as Vanbrugh himself noted: '[There] are Several Gentlemen in these Parts of the World that are possess'd with the Spirit of Building.' Among these amateurs was John Bourchier, who started work about 1710. He employed a local carpenter-architect, William Thornton, who had worked at Castle Howard, but Bourchier's time in Rome seems to have given him the self-confidence to design many of the details himself. Marriage to a wealthy heiress, Mary Bellwood, had provided the resources to build on the grand scale.

'All the world are running Mad after Building, as far as they reach.'
Sir John Vanbrugh, 1708

Later owners

1761–1827	The Earles
1827–1916	The Dawnays
1917–57	The Chesterfields

Three families owned Beningbrough after the Bourchiers. They comprehensively redecorated in the taste of their times, and transformed the garden and park. But they respected the outward appearance of the place. Beningbrough today remains John Bourchier's house.

(Below) The intertwined monogram 'JMB' (for the builder, John Bourchier, and his wife, Mary) appears in the carved-wood cresting of the overmantel in the Drawing Room

(Above) The north front

Drama and formality

Beningbrough's plain red-brick exterior, without pediment or portico, does not prepare you for the spatial drama of the Hall. It occupies the centre of the house, together with three other large and primarily architectural rooms – the Dining Room, Great Staircase and Saloon. Vaulted corridors in the style of Vanbrugh offer long vistas through the spine of the house and dizzying views down into the Hall from the first floor.

Stretching outwards from the centre of the south front are two matching suites of apartments – a series of progressively more private rooms where Bouchier (on the east side) and his more privileged guests (on the west) would have slept, dressed and received visitors. Bourchier would probably have furnished these rooms with Grand Tour pictures, china and the other luxury goods that were becoming increasingly available in York. Sadly, all the Bouchiers' movable furnishings have gone, but we can still get some idea of how richly the apartments would have been decorated from their extra-ordinary carved wood friezes. Created by Thornton and his team of Huguenot (French Protestant) craftsmen, they combine the virtuosity of Grinling Gibbons with the decorative inventiveness of William III's favourite designer, Daniel Marot.

(Right) The ground-floor apartments were arranged to create an eye-catching vista along the south front

In partnership

Beningbrough Hall and the National Portrait Gallery

Following the death of Lady Chesterfield, Beningbrough Hall passed to the National Trust in June 1958. As a fine example of a great Baroque house with exceptional wood carving, the Trust was keen to preserve and present the hall to the public. However, there was no endowment to cover running costs, and it was not until the mid-1970s that a proposal was developed to restore the interiors and transform Beningbrough into a major public attraction.

The first challenge for Beningbrough was that, when the Trust took the property on, it was almost entirely devoid of contents. The Trust had acquired Chesterfield portraits and some of the best furniture at the 1958 sale, but there was nowhere near enough to make a convincing display. It was here that the National Portrait Gallery stepped in. Following an existing partnership with the Trust at Montacute House in Somerset, where a number of Tudor and Jacobean paintings are displayed, the National Portrait Gallery arranged to lend Beningbrough 120 important eighteenth-

The Drawing Room has been refurnished with fine eighteenth-century pieces bought back for and bequeathed to Beningbrough

century portraits. The redisplay also benefited enormously from a generous loan of Chinese ceramics by the Ashmolean Museum in Oxford and a major bequest of period furniture from Lady Megaw.

The partnership between the National Trust and the National Portrait Gallery is now in its fourth decade. In 2003 the two organisations began fundraising for a major project to install a lift and refurbish the National Portrait Gallery's displays on the first and second floors of the house. After receiving generous support from the Heritage Lottery Fund, in 2006 Beningbrough Hall launched *Making Faces – Eighteenth Century Style*: a series of new, permanent, hands-on displays; an annually changing display of visiting portraits; a sound guide and computer interactives, which bring portraits to life for all the family.

(Left) This unusual portrait of the bedridden actress Peg Woffington is part of the National Portrait Gallery's loan to Beningbrough (NPG 650)

Fame and family

While few, if any, of the eighteenth-century celebrities depicted in the National Portrait Gallery's pictures – from King George I to the Yorkshire-born hero Captain Cook – would have visited Beningbrough, they would certainly have been known to its residents by reputation. Their presence here now allows Beningbrough to tell two interwoven tales: the local story of the house and its people and the national epic brought by the portrait collection. You can see how Beningbrough's eighteenth-century owners followed fashion in their clothes and in their taste for collecting blue-and-white porcelain – a trend that was encouraged by King William and Queen Mary. The portraits on display show many of the other leaders of fashion, politics and ideas – some of whom would have influenced the life and taste of the squires who lived at Beningbrough Hall.

Tour of the house

The Hall

The Great Hall was the traditional heart of the English country house. Bourchier modernised the form by giving it the classical grandeur of the Baroque palaces he had admired in Rome

The Hall was designed to impress and as a busy thoroughfare at the centre of the house.

The height of fashion

You step through the front door straight into a space that soars up through two floors of the building. Massive fluted pilasters reinforce the mood of monumental grandeur which characterises the entrance halls in the finest Yorkshire country houses of the period.

The hub of the house

The Hall connects all the parts of the house together. In the eighteenth century it would have been a place of constant activity, with servants passing to and fro. For this reason, it is sparingly furnished and decorated with hard-wearing materials. The Hall faces north and, despite the huge fireplace, can never have been warm. Visitors seated on the hard hall-chairs would not have been encouraged to linger.

Shades of stone

The chilly atmosphere is reinforced by the stony colours in which the room is decorated. When National Trust conservators stripped back centuries of paint from the plinths that support the pilasters, they discovered that they were made of solid York stone. This was used as the key for the creamy white colour in which the pilasters were redecorated. The walls behind were painted a greyer white. At the same time the Trust relaid the floor as it had been originally, with flagstones.

Master metalwork

Softening all this stony austerity is the curling wrought-ironwork of the grilles that front the first-floor balconies. They may be the work of

Representing royalty

William, Duke of Gloucester, the only surviving son of the future Queen Anne, died aged eleven in 1700. This made it likely that the English crown would pass to the Protestant Hanoverian descendants of James I. But this was not straightforward, for the exiled Catholic James II still had many supporters. When he died in 1701, his son James Edward Stuart – the Old Pretender – was proclaimed James III by Louis XIV of France. Attempts by James and his son, Charles Edward Stuart, to invade England in 1715 and 1745 left a deep mark on the national psyche. Their followers, the Jacobites, had considerable support among the Tory traditionalists, while the Protestant Hanoverians were supported by the Whigs.

For nearly 40 years the German-born Sir Godfrey Kneller (1646–1723) – who, like George I and George II, never lost his thick German accent – was Britain's leading portrait painter. Kneller's success lay in his continental training, his ability to manage a large and productive studio, and his reputation as the painter of many of Europe's monarchs. Indeed, from 1688 he was the Principal Painter to the English crown through each successive reign from William and Mary to George II.

NPG 2501

Kneller understood the important role portraits played for royalty. Official images, like those in the Hall, were not intended to depict individuals. Instead, by repeating poses and including the symbolic trappings of state – orb, sceptre and ermine robes – these portraits communicate abstract qualities like royal authority.

The portrait of George II's son, *Frederick, Prince of Wales* (1707–51) – by the York-based, Belgian-born artist Philip Mercier (1691–1760) – marks a departure from this tradition. Showing him in an elegant yet informal way, this image is as much about the Prince's taste as an art lover as it is about his fierce opposition to the King's politics.

the Derbyshire master-ironsmith Robert Bakewell (active 1707–52). The National Trust repainted them dark green on the basis of paint samples found under many later layers.

Sculpture

Portrait sculpture often decorated the entrance halls of Roman villas, which were the ultimate inspiration for Baroque houses like Beningbrough. The marble bust of ***Pope Clement XIV*** on the mantelpiece was carved in Rome in 1771 by the Irish sculptor Christopher Hewetson. The bust was bought by the Earles as a memento of their time in Rome in 1770–1, when Mrs Earle became pregnant. Clement gave her special permission to stay in a convent.

The Great Staircase Hall

> 'Because stayres at best are but an expedient to a defect, ... they should be made as easy, delightfull, and inviting as is possible.'
> Roger North, *On planning a country house*, c.1695–6

The staircase hall was conceived on the same scale as the entrance hall, and has a similar vaulted ceiling, which was inspired by Francesco Borromini's Collegio di Propaganda Fide (1647–64), one of the most monumental creations of the Roman High Baroque.

This is also a room of passage, providing a suitably dignified link between the Hall and State Apartment on the ground floor and the Saloon on the first floor, where large parties and formal dinners were held. The staircase was reserved exclusively for the family and their guests, who would have climbed it in formal procession on special occasions; servants would have had to use the back stairs. The shallow risers and two-metre-wide treads helped to make life easier for women ascending the stairs in the full skirts of the early eighteenth century.

The windows reveal Thornton's weaknesses as an architect: the rectangular frames of the sash-windows combine somewhat awkwardly with the round-headed window openings. The wall-mouldings seem to have been added about 1720, perhaps by John Bourchier's son, who may have found the bare walls too severe.

Staircase

The 'weightless' staircase soaring round three sides of the room is a typically Baroque effect. It was created with wrought-iron struts, which are cantilevered out from the walls and concealed within the oak construction. Unfortunately, the fabric is now so fragile that visitors can no longer use these stairs.

The ***balustrade*** is the finest feature of the staircase. The thin and beautifully carved balusters are similar to those at Treasurer's House in York (also the property of the National Trust), which may have been another Thornton commission. Even more remarkable are the pierced panels between them, which manage to simulate the delicacy of the finest wrought-iron work in the very different material of carved wood.

Furniture

The English ***mahogany commode***, c.1740, has lion-head's masks at the corners and particularly fine brass drawer handles. It may be the work of James Richards, who was the principal carver for the royal barge made for Frederick, Prince of Wales, whose portrait hangs in the Hall. Mahogany furniture was a fruit of empire. This fine-grained, deep red-brown wood was imported from the West Indian colonies from the early eighteenth century and remained the first choice of English cabinetmakers until the late eighteenth century.

Picture in focus

The North Front of Beningbrough Hall
By J. Bouttats and J. Chapman, 1751
This view of Beningbrough was painted for John Bourchier the Younger, who had inherited the estate from his father in 1736. Bourchier hung it over the chimneypiece in the library at Micklegate House, the new residence he had started building in York after his appointment as High Sheriff in 1749.

Such country-house views were popular among the landed gentry from the late seventeenth century. In some ways, they are like portraits – representations of their owners' wealth, taste and power. This painting may actually exaggerate the size of Bourchier's property, by including two wings on either side which may never have been built.

The painting is signed by two artists. Collaboration like this was not uncommon, since architectural painting and perspective were fairly specialised skills. Bouttats, who was of Dutch origin, probably painted the house, while the little-known Chapman painted the figures. Nice touches are the smoking chimneys and the open door and windows, all of which promise that visitors will receive a warm welcome.

The painting was purchased with funds provided by Mr I. F. Reddihough and the Art Fund.

The state bed in the Blue Bedroom

The Blue Bedroom

This room lies on the chilly, north side of the house and is less grandly decorated than the apartments along the south front. It may originally have been the Common Parlour, which would have been the family's everyday living and dining room. In the 1890s the Dawnays played billiards here. By the 1920s, it had become Lord Chesterfield's study.

In the 1970s the National Trust furnished the room as a bedroom to show the first of the two magnificent state beds at Beningbrough.

Bed

The 1680s state bed was probably the work of Francis Lapierre (active 1683–d. 1714), one of the leading French *émigré* upholsterers in late seventeenth-century Britain. Although Lapierre was a Catholic, he seems to have worked quite happily with the Huguenot *émigré* designers and craftsmen who dominated the upholstery trade. The bed was probably made for Holme Lacy in Herefordshire, and was sold by the Chesterfields when they moved from Holme Lacy to Beningbrough in 1917. It was acquired for Beningbrough with generous help from the National Art Collections Fund in 1980 in memory of Graham Baron Ash of Packwood, which is now also in the care of the National Trust. The blue damask is mostly modern, but may have been based on the original.

Picture in focus

Philip Dormer Stanhope, 4th Earl of Chesterfield (1694–1773)
By Allan Ramsay (1713–84), 1765 NPG 533
This politician and writer was an ancestor of the 10th Earl of Chesterfield, who bought Beningbrough in 1917. The 4th Earl was

noted for his opposition to the Whig policies of Prime Minister Sir Robert Walpole and for his celebrated *Letters to his Son* (1774). He was an art lover and an ardent Francophile, which may have encouraged him to choose the French-inspired Ramsay to paint this portrait.

Cross the corridor to reach the Closet, passing the late nineteenth-century conservatory.

The Closet

You enter the Closet from the back corridor, like the servants who would have attended the occupant as they dressed. It was the most private of the four rooms that originally formed the south-west apartment at Beningbrough, which would have been reserved for the Bourchiers' most honoured guests. The Closet served not only as a study, but also as a bathroom, giving its name to the modern water-closet (the cupboard originally concealed a close-stool or toilet). In the days before central heating, such small, easily heated rooms were particularly important in winter.

The ***corner fireplace*** seems to have been an English invention (Daniel Marot called it a *'cheminée à l'angloise'*). It had both a practical and a decorative function. It saved space, while throwing heat out into the room, and could also share a flue with fireplaces in adjacent rooms – in this case, the Dressing Room and the Drawing Room. The stepped shelves above it made the ideal place to display china.

The ***pine panelling*** would originally have been painted. It was stripped by the Chesterfields in the 1920s, when the fashion was for lighter wood.

> 'A closet, where the person, who is supposed of quality, to retire for devotion, or study, whilst the [bed]chamber is cleaned, or company present.'
>
> Roger North,
> *On planning a country house*, *c.*1695–6

Chinamania

To Bourchier and his contemporaries, China meant china: by the late seventeenth century the English East India Company was importing over a million pieces of Chinese porcelain a year. Many were simple cups and saucers for the other great eastern import – tea, which the Bourchiers would have drunk with their friends in rooms like this.

Queen Mary popularised the fashion for displaying china decoratively in the late 1680s. When Daniel Defoe visited her rooms in Kensington Palace, he was dismayed by 'the Custom or Humour, as I may call it, of furnishing houses with China-Ware, which increased to a strange degree afterwards, piling their China on the Tops of Cabinets, Scrutores [writing-desks], and every Chymney-Piece, to the tops of ceilings, and even setting up shelves for their China-Ware.' The porcelain shown on the Closet overmantel is Chinese early eighteenth-century *famille verte* (predominantly green-glazed) on loan from the Ashmolean Museum in Oxford.

The embroidered firescreen of c.1760 was designed to protect delicate complexions from the heat of a fire

The Dressing Room

A slightly larger room than the Closet, and again used by John Bourchier's guests when they wanted privacy. The Dressing Room and the Closet would have been furnished with the Bourchiers' most precious possessions, many of which may have come from the Far East. The National Trust has refurnished the Dressing Room to suggest something of its original richness.

A taste for the exotic

Lacquer was imported in smaller quantities than the other eastern luxuries – porcelain, tea, silk and chintz – but that gave it an even greater cachet. The Japanese and Chinese perfected the technique of decorating furniture with thin layers of black or red varnish, which were rubbed down and finally burnished to a lustrous sheen. The Chinese eighteenth-century ***black lacquer cabinet*** was the most popular type of lacquer furniture made specifically for the export trade. The doors open to reveal numerous small drawers, where prized curiosities could be kept.

The ***two panels*** hung flanking the cabinet are Coromandel lacquer, in which the design is incised into the surface. The name comes from trading posts on the Coromandel coast of India, through which such pieces were imported to Britain from China. These panels come from the screen shown in the Smoking Room; in the early eighteenth century whole rooms were sometimes lined with lacquer in this way.

English designers produced their own imitation lacquer furniture, using a technique known as japanning, which was popular from the late seventeenth century. The ***chairs*** and the ***stand*** are typical examples of their efforts.

> 'From the greatest gallants to the meanest cookmaids nothing was thought so fit to adorn their ... closets like China and lacquered ware.'
>
> John Pollexfen, 1698

57

The Drawing Room

The Drawing Room was originally two rooms: at the near end lay the State Bedchamber, and at the far end the Withdrawing Room. The ceiling beam marks the position of the former dividing wall, which was probably taken down in the 1830s, when the fashion for ground-floor bedrooms had passed, and there was a growing need for larger reception rooms on this floor.

Woodwork

The State Bedchamber and the Withdrawing Room were the two most important rooms in the State Apartment (see p. 20), and the outstanding quality of the carving reflects this. Especially fine is the carving of the frieze and overdoor surrounds in the nearer half of the room, where Thornton and his craftsmen excelled themselves. The frieze in the former State Bedchamber features tapering plinths, shells supported by palm fronds, vases and the initials 'JMB' for John and Mary Bourchier.

A royal cabinetmaker

Gerrit Jensen (active 1680–1715) was a Dutch or Flemish craftsman who was cabinetmaker to the English royal household during four reigns, from Charles II to Queen Anne. He was employed by the Crown 'making and selling of all Sorts of Cabbinets, Boxes, Looking Glasses and Stands Ebony Frames and for the Furnishing of all Sorts of Glase plates … and all things relating to the Cabbinet makers Trade.'

The Bourchiers' monogram appears once more in the cresting of the overmantel.

The frieze in the far section of the room (former Withdrawing Room) employs the motif of paired brackets of scrolling acanthus, which are somewhat similar to those supporting the cornice on the outside of the house.

The carving of the frames of the overdoors at each end of the room is particularly close in spirit to the ornament engravings of the French designer Jean Bérain and his Huguenot pupil Daniel Marot (see p. 21). Among Thornton's team of wood-carvers were two Huguenots, Jean Godier and Daniel Herve, who would almost certainly have looked at pattern books by Bérain and Marot.

As often happens in old houses, the panelling and wood-carvings are not all in their original position. They were moved around, and somewhat jumbled, during the alterations in the nineteenth century and again after 1917, when Lady Chesterfield also had the woodwork stripped of paint.

Furniture

The best pieces in the room are made of walnut, an easy-to-work, but durable native wood that was popular with English cabinetmakers between the Restoration in 1660 and the early eighteenth century.

Between the windows is a ***pair of English pier-glasses (mirrors) and tables*** of *c.*1690 in the style of the royal cabinetmaker Gerrit Jensen. They are decorated with 'seaweed' marquetry and 'oyster' veneer (the latter created by cutting a thin section through the timber at an oblique angle). The woods used are holly and princeswood, which was imported at great expense from central America and was reserved for the finest furniture. The cresting on the mirrors is a rare survival. Jensen held the royal monopoly on supplying mirror glass, which had become highly fashionable thanks to its wide-spread use at Versailles. It was a mark of genteel taste to have mirrors between the windows and over the chimneypiece in rooms used for receiving visitors.

The early eighteenth-century walnut ***bureau-bookcase*** is also decorated with oyster veneer and has particularly fine brass fittings.

(Right) The walnut pier-glass and matching table, c.1690, are in the style of Gerrit Jensen

(Far right) The early eighteenth-century 'oyster'-veneer bureau-bookcase

(Left) The carved-wood frieze in the Drawing Room incorporates shells, vases and palm fronds

John Montagu, 4th Earl of Sandwich; by Joseph Highmore, 1740. NPG 1977

The Drawing Room

Picture in focus

John Montagu, 4th Earl of Sandwich (1718–92)
By Joseph Highmore (1692–1780), 1740 NPG 1977

This portrait celebrates the young Lord Sandwich's intrepid voyage to the Middle East between 1737 and 1739 – a Grand Tour which went further afield than Italy, the destination for most of his contemporaries. He wears the exotic fur-lined costume that westerners sometimes adopted while travelling in the East. In the distance are the dome and minarets of Haghia Sophia in Istanbul and on the table drawings of the Pyramids.

As First Lord of the Admiralty in 1776–7, Sandwich was blamed for the poor performance of the British fleet in the war against the American rebels (1776–7). Nevertheless, he was dedicated to his post. Too busy to leave his desk (or gambling table), he invented the snack which still carries his name: the sandwich. The music-loving Sandwich was a patron of Handel (see p. 25).

Overdoors

It was fashionable in the early eighteenth century to incorporate family portraits into the fixed decoration of a room. Until recently, it was assumed that the overdoor paintings in this room were of John Bourchier and his family. In fact, they were introduced only in the 1890s, by Lewis Payn Dawnay, to fill gaps left when the originals were removed. They were left behind when the house was bought by the Chesterfields, who made the natural assumption that they represented the Bourchiers and their relations. The only Bourchier who can be firmly identified is John Bourchier the Younger, who was painted in 1732 by John Vanderbank. He commissioned the view of Beningbrough that has recently returned to the house (see p. 8).

(Right) This carved overdoor frames a portrait once thought to be of John Bourchier, builder of Beningbrough

Alexander Pope and the cult of celebrity

NPG 112

In his *Letters on England* (1733), the French philosopher Voltaire marvelled at the culture of modern fame that he had seen in England during his stay of 1726–9. He was particularly impressed by the way this popular fascination for celebrity also promoted painters and sculptors: 'What most encourages the arts in England is the consideration they enjoy; the portrait of the Prime Minister is over the mantelpiece … but I have seen Mr Pope's in a score of houses.'

Alexander Pope (1688–1744) dominated English poetry in the first half of the eighteenth century. His mastery of the English language enabled him to praise, mock or moralise on every subject with wit and elegance. Just as he paid unusually close attention to the production and appearance of his printed works, so he was acutely interested in controlling and disseminating his image. Of the nineteen major portraits of Pope, many were circulated in multiple copies, either in painted or printed versions. Revered as one of the greatest personalities of the age, Pope was the most frequently portrayed Englishman of his generation.

Having suffered from a spinal disease as a youth, Pope was sensitive about his image. (The painter William Hoare was able to record the poet's deformed back only by secretly making the little sketch illustrated on the right.) Still, there are many explanations for the wealth of portraits that exists: he had numerous admirers; many of his friends were artists who were keen to promote themselves by association, and Pope himself benefited from the publicity.

NPG 873

The portrait illustrated above is probably by Pope's friend and former art teacher, Charles Jervas (1675–1739). Painted about 1713–15, it is the earliest oil portrait of the rising star and one that carefully asserts the poet's ambitions. He is shown with head on hand and distant gaze – the first of many eighteenth-century portraits to use these conventions to suggest a thinker lost in reflection. The bust of Homer, to the left, is more specific: it refers to the translation of the ancient Greek that Pope was working on at the time. The woman in the background remains a puzzle. She may be Martha Blount, Pope's companion, but could also be an allegorical figure or muse.

The Dining Room

With its soberly panelled walls, the Dining Room marks a transition between the Hall and the two more intimate and richly furnished apartments that flank it. It occupies a key position at the centre of the south front, but, unusually for a Baroque house, the symmetry is not precise, as the two apartments are different lengths. As a result, the doors from the Hall and down to the garden are a little awkwardly placed in a corner of the room rather than at the centre.

This would originally have been called the Great Parlour. Because it was a semi-public room, it would have been sparsely furnished, with the chairs pushed back against the wall when not in use, as now. The term 'dining room' did not come into general use until the mid-eighteenth century, but this room would probably have been used for eating. Parlours were traditionally panelled rather than hung with fabric, which harboured the smell of stale food. It had certainly become the family's principal dining room by the nineteenth century, despite the distance from the kitchen.

Like the Hall, the Dining Room was originally painted a stony white. The National Trust painted it the present shade of grey green, which was found in another Baroque house, Boughton in Northamptonshire, to complement the Kit-Cat portraits hung here now.

The marble chimneypiece seems to have been copied by the Chesterfields from that in the Blue Bedroom. The overmantel with its boldly carved brackets and frame may, however, be original.

Jacob Tonson the younger, who inherited Kneller's famous series of portraits of the Kit-Cat Club and was also painted by him. *NPG 4091*

Furniture

The very fine walnut-veneered ***dining-chairs*** were made by Thomas Moore in 1734.

Kit-Cats and conversation

'Man is a sociable animal and we take all occasions and pretences of forming ourselves into those little nocturnal assemblies which are commonly known as clubs.' This was the critic Joseph Addison's view of the way masculine social life was increasingly shaped by clubs and societies. Usually meeting in taverns, like the one shown in this late seventeenth-century watercolour, members joined for mutual support and conversation.

The portraits in the Dining Room show members of the Kit-Cat Club, the most distinguished and influential club of its day. It was founded in the 1680s by leading Whig politicians and their supporters who shared a commitment to uphold the 'Glorious Revolution' of 1688 and the Protestant succession to the English throne. Their curious name – the Kit-Cat Club – came from the mutton pies that were made by Christopher Cat, the proprietor of the tavern where they met:

> Hence did th'Assembly's Title first arise,
> And Kit Cat Wits sprung from Kit-Cats Pyes.

(Right) In the late seventeenth century taverns and coffee houses were a popular venue for the growing network of male clubs like the Kit-Cat Club

The Kit-Cat's patronage of poets and playwrights such as Dryden and Congreve established their public reputation for culture and politeness. However, the club's riotous good humour can be judged from one bar bill of 1689, when the 55 members consumed around '20 gallons of claret, 6 of canary … 4 of white wine'! They were, nevertheless, the centre of opposition politics during Queen Anne's reign (1702–14).

The Duke of Somerset started the custom of presenting a portrait to the club's secretary, the publisher Jacob Tonson. In the first two decades of the eighteenth century, their resident artist – Sir Godfrey Kneller – painted nearly 40 club portraits. In doing so, he invented a new 'kit-cat' size which was larger than a standard bust portrait. This allowed Kneller to include one or more hands and a greater variety of natural poses. When hung together at Tonson's house, the overall effect was of a unified club, but one made up of individuals who each retain their character through distinct gestures, props and costumes.

Jacob Tonson retired around 1720 and passed his house and publishing business to his nephew, also called Jacob Tonson (over mantelpiece). Between 1731 and 1735 he published a series of engravings after Kneller's Kit-Cat Club portraits. Prints from this luxury volume, which are seen on the dining-table and in the State Dressing Room, were widely circulated and had a significant influence on later painters. The easy formality, assurance and mask-like features of Kneller's portraits typified the ideal of the early eighteenth-century gentleman.

The etiquette of access

The State Apartment

The State Apartment at Beningbrough was based on William and Mary's royal apartments at Hampton Court and Kensington Palace. In every age, political power has been synonymous with physical access to the ruler, which, as a result, has always been jealously regulated. The State Apartment was the seventeenth-century method of protecting the sovereign's privacy and defining the status of his courtiers. It comprised a linear series of increasingly exclusive rooms: semi-public audience chamber, withdrawing room, bedchamber, and finally and most private, a dressing room and closet. The further you were allowed to penetrate into the apartment, or the further the king emerged from his private chambers to greet you, the higher your status. Exactly the same principle applied at a less exalted level at Beningbrough, where John Bourchier 'kept estate' as the local representative of the crown.

The State Apartment would have been reserved for the use of Bourchier's most honoured guests, but because this apartment was dismantled in the 1830s (see p. 14), the National Trust has re-created the arrangement in the intact south-east apartment, which would probably have been used by Bourchier himself.

'It is usuall in great and noble appartments, to have an ordonnance [similar arrangement] beyond the withdrawing room, which is a state bedchamber, and inner rooms suitable to it.'

Roger North, *On planning a country house, c.*1695–6

The State Bedchamber

The State Bedchamber was the climax of the State Apartment. It was invariably the most richly decorated and furnished room in the entire suite, with upholstery predominating. Here the frieze shows Thornton's team of York carvers at their most inspired, with a continuous scrolling pattern of acanthus-leaf decoration, which frames four beautifully sculpted masks representing the seasons. The carved overdoors have superbly ornate surrounds, and the frames to the overmantel and the missing mirror below it are carved in exceptionally deep relief.

State bed

The focus of the State Bedchamber was the state bed, which was the great status symbol of the

(Right) The State Bedchamber

English Baroque house. Such beds were rarely slept in by the occupants of the State Apartment. Instead, they were kept on permanent display as a very visible sign of the family's power and wealth. A state bed was a hugely expensive purchase, sometimes costing as much as the rest of the furnishings combined. Particular attention was paid to the canopy or tester, not just as a decorative feature, but because of its symbolic function. When the monarch sat in state on his throne, it was beneath a canopy or 'cloth of estate', which came to represent royal authority in his absence. By extension, the state bed symbolised the power of the state.

This state bed is a particularly magnificent example of the upholsterer's art. Its wooden frame is comparatively crude, because it was entirely covered with fabric, which had to be skilfully fitted to the complex scalloped shapes of the canopy and headboard. The immense height of the bed gave it grandeur and allowed room for long bed-curtains with a very broad (and very expensive) repeat to the fabric pattern.

The bed was probably made in the early eighteenth century for James, 3rd Viscount Scudamore (1684–1716). A viscount's coronet appears on the fringed and braided backboard, and Scudamore was then the owner of Holme Lacy in Herefordshire, the house from which the bed was brought to Beningbrough by Lord Chesterfield about 1918. The bed was bought by the National Trust after Lady Chesterfield's death in 1957, when the contents of the house were sold.

Like the bed in the Blue Bedroom, it may be the work of the French master upholsterer Francis Lapierre and again it is in the style of his frequent collaborator, Daniel Marot (see box). Much of the crimson silk damask was replaced in the early twentieth century, when Morant & Co., leading dealers in historic furnishings, repaired the bed. At the time there was a revival of interest in Marot's work, which may have prompted the restoration work.

The bed still has its matching window pelmets (a very rare survival) and would probably have originally come with a suite of chairs and stools upholstered in the same fabric – part of the coordinated effect that Marot pioneered.

Daniel Marot – the first interior designer

Daniel Marot (1661–1752) was a key figure in creating, connecting and disseminating the court styles of France, Holland and England. He was born in Paris and trained with Louis XIV's influential designer of ornament, Jean Bérain. Religious persecution forced him to emigrate about 1685 to Holland, where he became chief designer to the Stadholder William III and his English consort Mary, creating the interiors of their summer residence at Het Loo. Marot followed William and Mary to England in the late 1680s, and was probably responsible for designing her magnificent state bed at Kensington Palace.

Marot had the apparently obvious, but new, idea of designing an interior as a decorative unity. He also disseminated his designs widely through engravings, which Thornton and his craftsmen would have looked at when seeking inspiration for the carved friezes at Beningbrough.

The State Dressing Room

This intimate room was reserved for the occupant of the bedchamber, and only close friends would have been invited to enter it. Somewhat at odds with the room's exclusive character is the view that it offers back along the entire length of the south front through the carefully aligned door openings. But in this case the Baroque love of such dramatic vistas outweighed the demand for privacy.

Portraits in print

The publishing industry in books and prints came of age in eighteenth-century Britain. The proliferation of engravings promoted public interest in the visual arts, brought art into the homes of ordinary people and gave rise to a new class of collectors and connoisseurs. It also provided national and international exposure for artists, especially in the first half of the century, when there were few formal opportunities to exhibit their work. Even a purchase was not necessary to see the

Blue and white

The Chinese blue-and-white Kangxi period (1662–1722) porcelain vases displayed in and on the corner chimney-piece are typical of those imported to Britain by Dutch traders following the foundation of the Dutch East India Company in 1602. Such was the demand for blue-and-white china that Dutch and English potters tried to simulate it. They had not yet discovered the secret of making porcelain, so resorted to the rather cruder technique of tin-glazed earthenware. Blue-and-white delftware (as it was known, after the chief Dutch centre of production) was hugely popular from the late seventeenth century, and took many forms, from delicate teaware to tall flower pyramids.

The State Dressing Room

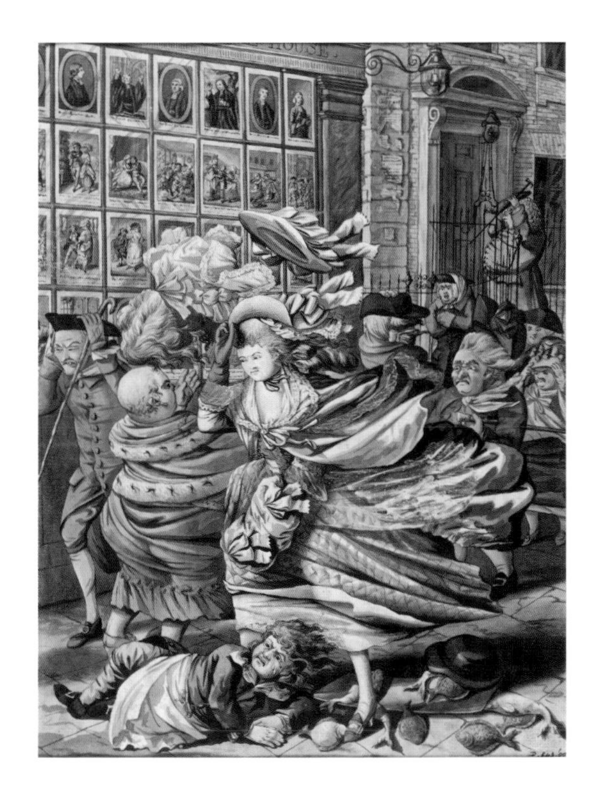

(Left) *A Windy Day in St Paul's Church Yard; by Robert Dighton, c.1783. The area around St Paul's Cathedral was full of bookshops displaying caricatures and portrait prints of the latest celebrities in their windows*

latest prints: *A Windy Day in St Paul's Church Yard* (*c*.1783) illustrates how printshop windows acted as galleries of the latest portraits.

Mezzotint engraving – which worked in light and shade rather than line – was the favourite medium for reproducing portraits. Artists were well aware of the importance of such prints and often formed professional partnerships with specific engravers. The relationship was a symbiotic one. The opportunity to engrave Kneller's Kit-Cat Club portraits put the young John Faber's name on the map, while the wide circulation of James Macardell's prints prompted Joshua Reynolds to declare: 'By this man I shall be immortalised.'

The State Closet

Both the State Dressing Room and Closet have richly carved overdoors and are panelled in pine, which was stripped by the Chesterfields in the 1920s.

The Closet would have been used for washing (the cupboard held a chamberpot) and private meals of the kind enjoyed by Lady Scudamore with her literary friends.

The Ground-floor Corridor

This corridor enjoys a vista that runs through the house parallel to that along the south front. The elliptical lobby was inspired by Borromini's Collegio di Propaganda Fide in Rome. The complex ceiling and door mouldings are made, not of plaster (as one would expect), but of wood – another demonstration of Thornton's skill as a carpenter-joiner.

The Smoking Room

Located close to the Hall and the service stair to the basement, this may have been the original Common Parlour or everyday living room (if the Blue Bedroom did not serve this purpose). But for the same reason it could have been John Bourchier's business room. A door to the left of the chimney provided access to an inner book room (not open), which suggests that this end of the ground floor may have been Bourchier's male domain, with his own apartment (bed-chamber, dressing room and closet) across the Corridor. The secondary stairs, which you are about to ascend, may therefore have provided Bourchier's access to his wife's apartment in the corresponding position upstairs.

Furniture

The three ***walnut and cane chairs*** date from about 1710. The caned chair was a genuine English innovation in the later seventeenth century, and virtually unknown in the rest of Europe. It used Rattan cane, a plant native to Asia which was strong, light and cheaper than upholstery (such chairs could be purchased for about 10 shillings). To add comfort, the chairs were often furnished with loose cushions called *squabs*.

The Saloon

This is the principal room on the first floor – the equivalent of the *Salone* in the Baroque palaces Bourchier had admired in Rome. He would probably have called it the Great Dining Room, using it for large gatherings – county balls, formal banquets, family parties and other occasions that needed space and a sprung floor. For this reason, it was thinly furnished until the nineteenth century, when Victorian clutter took over.

Like the Hall, this is a grand architectural space, articulated by the giant order of Corinthian pilasters, which make it resemble the garden front of Castle Howard turned inside out. The room was probably first painted silver grey. The Chesterfields produced an utterly different effect by decorating it in a bold shade of peacock blue. The National Trust revived the original scheme, suitably enriched with gold leaf on the pilasters and frieze.

The Grand Tour and Italian taste

When John Bourchier, the builder of Beningbrough Hall, departed for Italy in 1704, the Grand Tour was fast becoming an essential part of young noblemen's education. Italy, with its ancient Roman heritage, was viewed as the seat of classical civilisation, and a lengthy stay there was thought to encourage young men to develop good taste, culture, learning and civic virtue. Some, like Bourchier, studied art and architecture in Italy. Others were drawn to literature and philosophy. This was true of Anthony Ashley-Cooper, 3rd Earl of Shaftesbury (1671–1713), a classical scholar who visited Italy in 1688. This ***double portrait*** of him with his brother Maurice (1675–1726), wearing what was thought to be ancient Greek dress and set in a classical landscape with a temple of Apollo, was intended as a visual manifesto of their philosophical beliefs and brotherly affection.

By mid-century, many Britons were making the Grand Tour. Dean Tucker's *Instructions for Travellers* (1758) lists their reasons: 'First to make Curious Collections, as Natural Philosophers, Virtuosos or Antiquarians. Secondly to improve in Painting, Statuary, Architecture and Music. Thirdly to obtain the reputation of being Men of *Vertu* of an elegant Taste.' If the Grand Tour became a finishing school for young noblemen, it also turned England into a treasure-house of classical and contemporary art. Not only did the 'Milordi' – as the Italians mocked them – bring home antique Roman sculptures and Baroque paintings, they also commissioned portraits of themselves as souvenirs. Pompeo Batoni was the favourite artist for Grand Tour portraits, particularly for his ability to blend the trappings of ancient Rome with elegant portraits of his subjects. He was the choice of the statesman Augustus Henry Fitzroy, 3rd Duke of Grafton (1735–1811) and Philip Metcalfe (1733–1818), who is shown here complete with a distant view of the Colosseum in Rome.

NPG 5308

Furniture

Appropriately for a Rome-inspired room, the furniture is Roman. The ***giltwood chairs*** with griffin arms come from a suite of over 70 designed about 1805 by the brothers Dionisio and Lorenzo Santi of Rome. They are said to have been a present from the French Emperor Napoleon to his uncle, Cardinal Fesch, who was French ambassador to the Vatican. They were later owned by the important English collector and furniture designer Thomas Hope of Deepdene (1769–1831).

Overdoors

They depict ***stag hunting in Galtres forest***. The medieval Beningbrough estate lay within this ancient forest, over which the King had hunting and other rights. The Bouchiers were hereditary rangers of Galtres, and these paintings are among the few survivals of their collections at Beningbrough.

Picture in focus

George Frideric Handel (1685–1759)
Attributed to Balthasar Denner (1685–1749), 1726–8 NPG 1976

Born in Saxony, Handel settled in London in 1712. For nearly 50 years he poured out operas, oratorios and concertos. His *Messiah*, first performed in Dublin in 1742, was a national institution within his lifetime. This picture was probably painted for Handel by Balthasar Denner, a fellow German. It is the earliest portrait of the composer.

Lady Chesterfield's Rooms

The next three rooms together form the third of Beningbrough's apartments, occupying the south-west corner of the first floor.

Lady Chesterfield's Bedroom

Lady Chesterfield used this as her bedroom from 1917; indeed, it has always been a bedroom.

Once again the room is panelled with a decorative frieze, directly inspired by an engraving in Daniel Marot's *Nouveau Livre d'Ornaments*, which was published in The Hague in 1700. The overdoors are indebted to Borromini.

The simply moulded chimneypiece is made from Derbyshire fossil marble and may be the original.

Bed

This is the third of the Holme Lacy state beds now at Beningbrough. Although more modest than those on the ground floor, it still has a very elaborate upholstered backboard. The crimson silk damask was renewed in the 1920s by Lenygon & Morant, who also supplied the matching window curtains and the pelmets, which were skilfully created from scratch in the style of Daniel Marot.

Furniture

The seventeenth-century desk is decorated with metal inlay on a red-painted background in the style of André-Charles Boulle, cabinetmaker to Louis XIV. The type is known as a *bureau mazarin* after the French king's chief minister.

The French travelling toilet set was used by Lady Chesterfield.

Picture in focus

Margaret 'Peg' Woffington (1720?–60)
By an unknown artist, *c.*1758 NPG 650
This unusual sick-bed portrait shows the celebrated Irish actress 'Peg' Woffington after she collapsed and was paralysed in 1757.

During the previous twenty years she had made her name in comedy. She was notorious for bitter rivalries with other actresses – even stabbing one in a performance – and for her supposed love affair with Britain's leading actor, David Garrick.

Lady Chesterfield's Dressing Room

This room matches the Dressing Room in the south-west apartment immediately below and is fitted out in the same way with panelling and a corner fireplace. Here, however, Lady Chesterfield decided not to strip the white painted panelling. In the 1970s the National

The last of the line

Enid, Lady Chesterfield (1878–1957) was the daughter of a wealthy Hull shipping owner. In 1900 she married the 10th Earl of Chesterfield, who was more than twice her age. They bought Beningbrough in 1917, bringing with them many of the historic furnishings of Holme Lacy, the Chesterfields' ancestral home, which they had sold eight years before. Lady Chesterfield comprehensively redecorated Beningbrough and furnished it in grand style. After Lord Chesterfield's death in 1933, she lived on alone in the house, devoting most of her energies to breeding racehorses. She had no children and was the last private owner of Beningbrough.

Trust's adviser on decoration, John Fowler, suggested picking out the mouldings in blue to match the blue-and-white porcelain displayed on the chimneypiece (from the Ashmolean Museum loan and Bushell bequest). Fowler's scheme was generally considered a failure, and so the Trust has repainted the room in shades of white.

Pictures in focus

Prince Charles Edward Stuart (1720–88) and *Henry Benedict Maria Clement Stuart, Cardinal York* (1725–1807)
Studio of Antonio David (1698–1750), *c.*1729–32 NPG 434, 435

Grandson of the Catholic James II, Prince Charles was commonly known as 'Bonnie Prince Charlie' or the 'Young Pretender'. In 1745 he led the abortive uprising to claim the British crown. After the failure of this rebellion, his younger brother, Henry, abandoned the Jacobite cause and entered the Church, becoming a cardinal in 1747. When he died, he bequeathed the Stuart crown jewels to the future George IV – an act that symbolically ended the Jacobite cause. These paintings were done in Italy, where the children's family was in exile, to send to Jacobite sympathisers either in Britain or France.

Admiral Edward 'Old Grog' Vernon (1684–1757)
By Thomas Gainsborough (1727–88), *c.*1753
NPG 881

Vernon captured the Spanish colonial possession of Portobello (now in Panama) during the War of Jenkins' Ear in 1739. His greatest claim to fame, however, was his 1740 order that his crew's rum ration should be diluted with water and should have lemon juice added to prevent scurvy. The rest of the Navy rapidly followed his lead, calling the new drink 'grog' after Vernon's nickname.

Lady Chesterfield's Bathroom

Lady Chesterfield transformed this closet into a modern bathroom in the 1920s. The decorative scheme, of stippled apricot above veined black marbling, may have been carried out by Lenygon & Morant.

The carved marble basin may be a rare surviving eighteenth-century feature, perhaps moved here from the empty niche in the lobby outside. ***The sunken bath*** is an unusually advanced feature for the 1920s.

(Left) Lady Chesterfield's Dressing Room
(Right) Lady Chesterfield's Bathroom

Making Faces

The National Trust, working in partnership with the National Portrait Gallery, and with the support of the Heritage Lottery Fund, refurbished, redisplayed and enhanced access to Beningbrough Hall in 2006. The result is *Making Faces – Eighteenth Century Style*, which includes an innovative series of interactive galleries, new graphic and audio interpretation, and the installation of a lift.

On the first floor, *Making Faces* presents three new interpretation galleries in historic rooms that have been restored and fully opened to the public for the first time. These new galleries provide opportunities to enjoy the full range of the National Portrait Gallery collection – from Tudor times to the present; in the new IT study-room where the Gallery's *Portrait Explorer* is installed; and in *Visiting Portraits*, an annually changing, in-focus display. Finally, you can get to grips with historic portraiture in *Family Matters*, the first of the new interactive galleries. This offers a hands-on introduction to reading historic portraiture through a series of fun activities based around three family portraits.

Making Faces continues on the top floor, where two more interactive galleries – *Getting the Picture* and *Turning Heads* – bring portraits to life. In *Getting the Picture*, high-and low-tech activities include *Virtual Portrait*, *A Portrait Sitting* and *Finishing off*; these let you commission an eighteenth-century-style portrait from a virtual artist, make your own living portrait, and discover the tricks that artists employed to get the job done. *Turning Heads* introduces the making and meaning of portrait sculpture in marble, terracotta and bronze. Decide whether you would prefer your portrait in paint or sculpture, and try your hand at modelling. See how different materials change the way a portrait works, and explore sculpture by touch to find all the hidden details. There is also a pre-school portrait playroom.

(Right) Christopher Anstey with his Daughter; by William Hoare, c.1776-8. NPG 3084

Family Matters

Britain entered a period of economic and political stability after the South Sea Bubble financial crash of 1720. With prosperity came increased social mobility and the rise of a new 'middling sort' – a large and varied group of provincial gentry and the wealthy merchants with whom they intermarried. Confident and prosperous, this 'middling sort' commissioned portraits and was drawn to a new style – the

(Above) The Shudi Family; by Marcus Tuscher, c.1742. NPG 5776

conversation-piece – which was enjoyed by both merchants and aristocrats.

Described at the time as 'pictures in little', conversation-pieces tended to be small and well suited to hanging in a town house as opposed to a country mansion. Rather than being simple portrait heads, these new pictures usually represented a family or group of friends engaged in informal activities: playing cards, drinking tea or making music. A fashionable setting – whether indoors or outdoors – and a fine array of props were also important, and artists paid special attention to the family's material possessions as evidence of their taste and wealth. The relationships between people were as crucial as their luxury commodities – silver chocolate-pots, Chinese porcelain or Turkish carpets, as these suggested prosperity, relaxed confidence and family harmony.

Children had a key role to play both in reality and its representations. Like the young Joshua Shudi, they were increasingly allowed their own identity rather than being miniature adults. But standing close to his father, Joshua still represents the continuation of the Shudi line and the descent of their property. In the 1750s and 1760s the acceptance of the French philosopher Rousseau's theories on childhood as a special state encouraged a new more sentimental and relaxed attitude towards children. It was then that portraits such as *Christopher Anstey with his Daughter* (c.1776–8) began to celebrate a more affectionate and natural interaction between children and their parents.

The Shudi Family

By Marcus Tuscher (1705–51), c.1742

NPG 5776

Of Swiss origin, Burkat Shudi (1702–73) settled in London in 1718 and soon established himself as a leading harpsichord-maker. This conversation-piece tells us much about the family and their aspirations. The painting is set in their newly purchased Soho town house. Shudi's profession and standing are suggested as he tunes a magnificent harpsichord; on the wall behind him a mezzotint engraving acknowledges his patron, Frederick, Prince of Wales (see p. 6). This portrait probably celebrates the inheritance of his wife Catherine's family estate: she is thought to be holding a copy of the will.

Portraits tell Stories

Why have a portrait? In the past, people had many of the same reasons for commissioning portraits that we still have today. Portraits record and celebrate key moments in our family and professional lives: graduation, marriage, professional status, special journeys or important birthdays.

The first photographs were taken in the 1830s. Before that, oil portraits, watercolour miniatures and engraved reproductions were the main way of recording a person's appearance. Such portraits could then act as a substitute for the sitter; perhaps when a husband had gone to war, or as a keep-sake between separated lovers. Portraits often caught subjects in the prime of life, outliving them as they aged and died. People frequently bequeathed their portraits to children or friends – to keep their memories alive. Dynastic and commemorative collections were formed to record ancestry, political allegiances or social and intellectual networks. Founded in 1856, the National Portrait Gallery continues these traditions – but on a national scale – in collecting portraits of people who have made significant contributions to Britain's history and culture.

A portrait is more than a simple likeness of a person. Its composition and appearance can be subjective, biased, flattering and even deceitful. Portraiture is the result of an exchange between artist, sitter and occasionally a separate patron, each of whom has an interest in the finished work. While the best artists convey something of the sitter's character and beliefs, achievements and ambitions, the painting's own history tells us the way a portrait was perceived and used by its owners and viewers. As a result, portraits tell stories about sitters, artists and their public.

Thomas Day (1748–89)
By Joseph Wright of Derby (1734–97), 1770
NPG 2490

Thomas Day was the ultimate eighteenth-century 'man of feeling'. A follower of Rousseau's philosophies, he devoted himself to charity, the well-being of others, and the promotion of radical social reform. He aspired to live an ascetic and reclusive life but became a famous, best-selling author with his sentimental children's book *The History of Sandford and Merton* (1783–9) – an instructive tale of two boys whose escapades teach them that moral behaviour leads to virtuous manhood.

Day must have been one of Joseph Wright's most awkward and reluctant sitters: he seldom

(Right) Thomas Day; by Joseph Wright of Derby, 1770. NPG 2490

washed his hair and cared nothing for modern fashion or portraiture. Nevertheless, Wright conveyed Day's identity as a 'sentimental' man at one with nature. The totally imaginary Van Dyck silk suit removes him from the everyday and brings an intense reflective light to the figure; this underlines Day's enlightenment against a stormy background. Showing Day gazing into the distance with a 'meditative and melancholy air', Wright's portrait tells us that Day's heart and mind are on higher matters.

This is the only portrait of Thomas Day. He was probably persuaded to sit for it by his close friend, Richard Lovell Edgeworth, who introduced him to Rousseau's writings. Day died in 1789, a martyr to his own theories – having been thrown from a horse he was trying to tame through kindness. Three weeks later, Edgeworth offered the portrait to Day's distraught wife as a memorial of their friendship.

The Three Ages of Man: William Augustus, Duke of Cumberland from childhood to middle age
(Top left) Aged about seven; by Charles Jervas. NPG 802; (bottom left) Aged about 28; studio of David Morier. NPG 537; (below) Aged 38; studio of Sir Joshua Reynolds. NPG 625

Getting the Picture

In 1712 *The Spectator* commented that 'England is confessed to abound in Face-Painters'. Confronted by an ever-growing community of portrait painters, Sir Joshua Reynolds later lamented that the population of London could provide a living 'for eight painters only'. These comments show that throughout the eighteenth century portrait painting was a competitive, commercial business in a buyer's market. Special social skills and professional ability were essential to getting ahead.

(Above)
A Family Piece.
An engraved caricature of a family sitting for their portrait; by William Henry Bunbury, 1781.
NPG D21380

(Left)
Susannah Cibber;
by Thomas Hudson,
c.1749.
NPG 4526

From Kneller to Reynolds and beyond, success as a portrait painter depended not just on the ability to capture likeness. Portrait painters had to cope with intense psychological interaction and with constant public performance. While they had to tread a fine line between servile flattery and being an equal of their sitter, confident social skills were not enough. To flourish, a portrait painter had to combine hard work, skill, creativity, good business sense and entrepreneurship to attract new clients and stay in the public eye.

No one understood the importance of social position to their career better than Reynolds. In 1760 he invested in a 'superior mansion' in Leicester Fields in London – a fashionable address which acted as a reassurance and guarantee for his more elevated patrons. To this property Reynolds then added a spacious studio, elegant reception rooms and a gallery for the display of his work. As his business and status grew, the house became a fashionable meeting-place. As Reynolds ensured that sitting for a portrait was a sociable activity, people brought their friends and family. Others dropped in to see works on display, choose poses and costumes for their own portraits, and make appointments for sittings.

One way of dealing with a heavy workload was to delegate parts of the portrait. Kneller's studio was a 'busy manufactory' with a production-line where assistants added costumes, backgrounds and other components to Kneller's canvasses. By the 1730s and 1740s, the demand for portraiture at all levels had grown, and Joseph van Aken (*c.*1699–1749), a Flemish immigrant, was Britain's leading independent drapery painter.

(Right) William Pulteney, 1st Earl of Bath; by Sir Joshua Reynolds, 1761. NPG 337

He specialised in adding the 'silks, satins, velvets and embroideries' to canvasses commenced by better-known artists like Allan Ramsay (1713–84) and Thomas Hudson (1701–79). Van Aken's anonymous contributions brought him great wealth, and led Horace Walpole to complain: 'Just as everybody in England has their picture painted, so almost every painter's work is painted by van Aken.' But the practice did not die with van Aken; Reynolds also employed drapery painters to finish portraits once his sitters had gone. This was the case with *William Pulteney, 1st Earl of Bath* (1761), as the sitter wrote indignantly:

> I have discovered a secret by being often at Mr Reynolds, that I fancy, he is sorry I should know. I find that none of these great Painters finish any of their Pictures themselves. The same Person ... works for Ramsay, Reynolds, and another called Hudson, my Picture will not come from that Person till Thursday night, and on Friday it will be totally finished, and ready to send home.

Turning Heads

The portrait bust is one of the most common forms of sculpture, still frequently found in public institutions, libraries, country houses and art galleries. Despite this ubiquity, it is now the most neglected type of portraiture – difficult to understand or even to look at. To bring sculpture back to life, *Turning Heads* invites visitors to get to grips with the making, meaning and significance of portrait busts in the eighteenth century.

In the first decades of the century most sculptors were engaged in producing funeral monuments. Until the arrival of the Flemish sculptor John Michael Rysbrack (1694–1770) in 1720, there was little demand for sculpted portraits from life. But by 1747 a directory of London trades noted:

> The taste of Busts ... prevails much of late years, and in some measure interferes with Portrait Painting: The Nobility now affect to have their Busts ... rather than sit for their Pictures, and the Fashion is to have their Apartments adorned with Bronzes and Figures in Plaister and Wax.

The majority of portrait busts were actually carved in marble or cast in bronze. The durability of these materials was intrinsic to the demand for portrait sculpture. As was the inescapable association with classical Roman busts, which sculptors often reinforced by portraying their subjects in togas. Another common approach, again suggesting a classical and timeless ideal, was the bare torso, like that of *Captain James Cook* or the architect *James Wyatt*. More unusual was sculpted 'undress', like *Isaac Ware's* open shirt and soft cap, which celebrated a man of thought rather than action.

Captain James Cook (1728–79)
By Lucien le Vieux (active 1790), 1790
Marble bust NPG 984

The explorer and circumnavigator Captain Cook was the son of a Yorkshire labourer who learned his seamanship on small East Coast trading ships. Noted for his mathematical and business acumen, Cook was chosen to command the *Endeavour* in 1768, although he was then only a warrant officer. He made three voyages of discovery to the South and North Pacific – charting land, sea and stars – and was the first British captain to land in Australia. He was killed in Hawaii during a skirmish.

This idealised bust is unlike any authentic image of Cook. We know that it is intended to portray him from the inscription on the base: JACQUES COOK/ NÉ DANS LE COMTÉ/ D'YORK EN 1728/ MORT DANS L'ISLE/ D'OWHYHÉE EN

(Right) The sculptor John Michael Rysbrack; attributed to John Vanderbank, c.1728. NPG 1802

1779 ('James Cook, born in the county of York[shire] in 1728, died on the island of Hawaii in 1779'). The severe antique style, with short hair and bare torso, would have been understood as presenting Cook as an illustrious hero of everlasting reputation.

This sculpture is based on one carved by Augustin Pajou, in 1788, for Jean-Joseph Laborde, a wealthy French financier. Laborde had earned his fortune in maritime trade and was fascinated by navigation and discovery. This passion led him to commission Pajou's sculpture for a Neo-classical cenotaph to Captain Cook – one of the several follies he erected in his English-style pleasure gardens at the château of Méréville near Paris. Cook had already been commemorated with a monument at Stowe in Buckinghamshire, one of the landscape gardens that inspired Méréville.

(Above) Captain James Cook; by Lucien le Vieux, 1790. NPG 984
(Left) The Cook Monument at Stowe

The Laundry

You descend to the ground floor via a servants' stair or the new lift, and leave the house through the front door. The arch to the left under the Bell Tower leads to the laundry yard.

Before the restoration in the late 1970s, the laundry yard was overgrown and surrounded by derelict buildings. The yard has been recobbled, and the coach-house and Laundry restored. The latter contains its nineteenth-century arrangement of 'wet' and 'dry' rooms.

The Wet Room

The smaller Wet Room, to the right, has two boilers heated by a fire below. The larger one, into which water was pumped, was probably used for boiling clothes, while the smaller one provided water for general washing. The wooden sinks originally had copper taps.

The wooden implement, resembling a four- or six-legged stool with a handle and crossbar is a ***Dolly***, which was twisted backwards and forwards in a wooden or zinc dolly tub to force soapy water through dirty clothes.

The ***Poss Stick***, made from a solid piece of wood and widening to a cylinder with four cuts, beat the dirt out of clothes. It was superseded by the copper bell-shaped ***Posser***, which cleaned by suction when moved up and down in the wash tub.

The fluted zinc ***washing boards*** were used for scrubbing very dirty clothes.

The Dry Room

In the Dry Room, to the left, is an iron-framed ***mangle*** with two rollers. It could be used for either wringing wet clothes or pressing dry ones. In the centre of the room the ***box mangle***, containing stones, pressed large damp sheets or tablecloths with wooden rollers fitted under the box. The room also includes a selection of box, flat and polishing ***irons***, and a ***goffering machine*** for giving a neat finish to frills. To the left of the boiler are two more hand-operated ***washing machines*** dating from the early twentieth century.

(Left) The Wet Room
(Right) The Dry Room

The grounds and garden

Beningbrough lies in the fertile flood plain of the River Ouse, where it joins the River Nidd in the midst of the Vale of York. The origins of the estate are obscure, but undoubtedly ancient, dating back at least to the possession of the estate by the monks of St Leonard's Hospital, York, in the twelfth century. The medieval park contained areas used for arable farming and garden produce, an agricultural enclave in the heart of the royal Forest of Galtres. In the seventeenth century canals were dug across part of this flat landscape, but otherwise it probably changed little until the building of the present house, when the landscape was formalised by the planting of grand avenues centring on the house. The late eighteenth and early nineteenth centuries saw the removal of the formal elements of the landscape, which was altered to the English style of 'Capability' Brown and Humphry Repton. In Victorian times, William Henry Dawnay created intimate flower gardens around the house. The Chesterfields kept the garden in good order from 1917 until the outbreak of the Second World War.

The medieval estate

In 1284 the brethren of St Leonard's were granted permission to enclose a further 100 acres of their own land and 56½ acres of adjoining woodland to create the 'new park of Beningburg', an area which appears on old maps as the Old Deer Park north-east of the house, beyond the present park. This brought the area of land farmed by the brethren to some 540 acres, of which 366 were arable land and pasture, a small part being meadow mown for hay, and an area near the Grange – the building from which the estate was run – being used for orchards and kitchen gardens. A recent archaeological survey has revealed possible signs of the

The Saloon overdoors depict stag hunting in the ancient royal Forest of Galtres, which once surrounded the Beningbrough estate

An intriguing sketch of 1719–23 made by Samuel Buck survives showing the eastern half of a parterre design which may or may not have existed south of the house. Buck's sketch shows a design of four large compartments divided by a broad path running southwards from the house and an east–west cross path terminated by a splendid gate. The compartments near the house would have been *parterres de broderie*, elaborately scrolled Baroque designs of box edging possibly infilled with coloured gravels. The two further compartments are shown as beds of simpler shapes, which would also probably have been box-edged. Each compartment is surrounded by a narrow border or *plate bande*, probably edged with box, planted with flowers and punctuated with topiary cones of evergreens. At the far end of the garden is 'a fine channel' or canal running east–west, which seems to have borders and a path on either side. (Recent archaeology has suggested that this canal may have been a survivor of the seventeenth-century garden that surrounded the Elizabethan house.) Railings are shown separating the garden from the park. The extent of the garden appears to be considerable, stretching well beyond the position of the present ha-ha.

monastic gardens in the park just to the south of the present garden.

The ancient origins of the estate and the fact that it has never been entirely cleared of trees and woodland have ensured a rich diversity of flora and fauna. Insects associated with ancient woodland are well represented, including a spider-hunting wasp (*Dipogon subintermedius*), one of the species of spectacular Red Cardinal beetles and the Purple Hairstreak butterfly.

The early eighteenth-century garden

When the present house was completed in 1716, the formal style of landscape design still reigned supreme. Early maps show the grand avenues which were typical of the period: a single avenue of Common Lime (*Tilia* × *europaea*) marched away from the house to the north; the walk along the south front of the house was extended to the west by another avenue, combining with a further three to the south-west (towards the Nun Monkton ferry), south and south-east to create a *patte d'oie*, or goose-foot, of allées, a feature often found in landscapes of the time, most notably at Hampton Court. The route from the ferry would have been an important access, and boats would still have been a convenient means of transport at this period, particularly for visitors coming from York.

The Earles

When the estate passed to the last of the Beningbrough Bourchiers, Margaret, and her husband Giles Earle, in the early 1760s, avenues and formal gardens were out of fashion. It is likely that such young occupants, with every expectation of seeing new planting reaching maturity, would have wanted to make changes, but it seems that the Earles were cautious in their approach, leaving the avenues perhaps as a nurse for new planting or to grow sufficiently to produce saleable timber. The avenues still appear in Jeffrey's map of England (1767–70).

The Newton entrance lodge is an almost exact copy of one built at Thirkleby Hall near Thirsk in the 1790s for Sir Thomas Frankland and probably designed by James Wyatt. It is likely that much of the landscaping of the entrance drive and the north park (which was added to the estate in 1810) dates from around this period. Successful landscaping on such a flat site is difficult, but the apparent lack of distinction of the design suggests it was made by the Earles themselves or their land agent rather than a professional landscaper. The rather straight drive from Newton gate seems to have aimed in a rather unsatisfactory way at the west pavilion rather than the house itself. These shortcomings may have led to the reinstatement of the north avenue early in the twentieth century, keeping the house hidden until its dramatic appearance framed by a lime avenue.

Earle is portrayed unflatteringly in a novel about Beningbrough written by J. L. Armstrong in 1836; referring to the estate as it was in the late eighteenth century, Armstrong writes of tall elms east of the hall and of a beech avenue beside the Ouse which may have been one of those shown in Jeffrey's map or perhaps the wooded walk which ran round the perimeter of the estate. The southern section of this walk, known as The Belt, is unusual in that then, as now, it completely blocked views to the river and the countryside beyond.

A French visitor in June 1768 describes the gardens:

Walked in the gardens which are very pretty with water and the river below. Fine bowling green, beautiful menagerie with pheasants, fine lawn and bosquets of foreign trees, heated glasshouses for pineapples. Magnificent outbuildings, beautiful stables, beautiful allée of oaks in a field in front of the house – with irregular clumps of trees but making a charming effect to either side of the allée. Beautiful English greenery which no other country can match.

The park to the south of the house still reflects the informal planting of the late eighteenth and early nineteenth centuries

The Dawnays

With the death of Margaret Earle in 1827, Beningbrough passed to her distant cousin, the Rev. William Henry Dawnay, later 6th Viscount Downe. Dawnay appears to have been particularly active in instigating new planting in the following years, and many existing trees seem to date from this period.

Thomas Foster (1798–1866) worked as Head Gardener for Dawnay from 1824, apparently coming to Beningbrough in 1827, when Dawnay inherited. He evidently brought the gardens to a high standard of horticultural excellence, winning frequent prizes at the York Horticultural Society shows, particularly for soft fruit, vegetables and dahlias. His most outstanding success was the raising in about 1835 of two new varieties of glasshouse grape from a cross between 'Black Morocco' and 'White Sweetwater'. 'Lady Downe's Seedling', a sweet and richly flavoured white, is often rated the finest late-keeping glasshouse grape, ripening in August but keeping on the vine in good condition until the following March. 'Foster's Seedling' is also white, sweet and well-flavoured and perhaps the best early grape; it was traditionally produced in royal glasshouses for Queen Mary, to be presented to her each year on her birthday, 26 May. Both varieties now grow in the vinery in the Walled Garden.

The estate map of 1841 records tree-planting predominantly in the informal landscape style, although with several straight lines of trees (perhaps not avenues, but the remains of old hedgerows). The house and kitchen garden are shown surrounded by typical Victorian pleasure grounds (although these might date from the time of the Earles). The Walled Garden appears with an extension or 'slip' to the south. The area south and east of this and bounded by the ha-ha is intersected by paths and planted with trees. Most of the trees which have been dated by ring-counting were planted in 1830–60.

In 1848, two years after the estate had passed to Lord Downe's son, Payan Dawnay, Beningbrough was surveyed for the first Ordnance Survey map, which appeared in 1852. South of the Walled Garden, the South Bower is shown for the first time, while the area to the east is described as the American Garden, also with its own bower. American gardens became a popular feature in the early nineteenth century, but paradoxically contained a wide variety of lime-hating plants from countries other than North America, particularly rhododendrons.

An account of the garden written in spring 1855 by Michael Saul, Head Gardener at Stourton Castle, mentions a number of exotic trees such as a large arbutus and recent introductions, for instance a Deodar (1831), Californian Redwood (*Sequoia sempervirens*, 1841), *Cryptomeria japonica* (1842) and Bhutan Cypress (*Cupressus torulosa*, 1824). In the conservatory (not the present building, although it may have been on the same site) were cinerarias, azaleas, Cape heaths, *Primula sinensis* and *Lachenalia tricolor*. A greenhouse was also stocked with flowering shrubs, perhaps to supply the conservatory, and there were also three stove houses of tropical plants, a peach house and a pine house, in which some orchids were grown alongside the pineapples.

The Walled Garden was stocked with the choicest fruit, including a particularly good range of pear varieties such as 'Marie-Louise', 'Winter Nelis', 'Easter Beurré' and 'Beurré Rance'. This was clearly a garden in which botanical diversity and the highest horticultural standards were encouraged by interested owners and made possible by highly skilled staff.

(Right) The coat of arms of the Dawnay family appears on the gates of the Walled Garden

Lewis Payn Dawnay

Lewis Payn Dawnay inherited the estate from his uncle in 1891; the following years saw substantial changes. In 1894 alone 11,000 trees were planted, and various alterations were made to the garden and grounds. The ha-ha south of the house was curved outwards to extend the lawn; two skating ponds were made; the low wall of the North Forecourt was built and the drives realigned to allow the replanting of the North Avenue, regrettably with Broadleaved Lime, a species less tolerant of the high water table here than the original Common Lime. The failure of many of these limes in the avenue has necessitated their replacement with the more vigorous 'Pallida' form of Common Lime.

The 1916 sale catalogue provides the most comprehensive insight into the estate at that time. It encompassed 33 farms, over 6,000 acres and most of the villages of Newton and Shipton. The Home Farm included a large complex of mainly nineteenth-century buildings. Other buildings within the park included the racket court built in 1901 and a castellated water tower situated on top of an artesian well on the banks of the River Ouse. With its giant pilasters and castellated parapet, the tower was obviously designed to be enjoyed as a park building. The sale catalogue describes a splendid dahlia border in the walled garden slip, continuing the tradition established by Thomas Foster for growing them, and a rose garden in the area now called the Cherry Lawn.

(Right) The west formal garden

The Chesterfields

The mansion, home farm and park were eventually bought by Lord and Lady Chesterfield in 1917. The Chesterfield Stud became the main enterprise of the estate, centred on the Home Farm, and the buildings near the Tench Pond were turned into a horse surgery.

Although they made few changes to the gardens, it seems that the Chesterfields were keen gardeners, as indicated by several plants named in their honour: Lady Chesterfield was commemorated by a carnation and a narcissus, and both she and the Earl had pelargoniums named after them; sadly, none of these seems to have survived. The Countess restored the two small formal gardens on either side of the south terrace and took particular pride in the border south of the Walled Garden, which was always at its best when visitors came to stay during the St Leger meeting each September.

The west formal garden

The National Trust

During the Second World War ornamental gardening virtually stopped, and the south lawn was ploughed up to grow cabbages and potatoes. When the National Trust accepted Beningbrough in 1958, the garden was in a fairly rundown state. The garden staff had been reduced from three to one, and the Walled Garden was rented out to a market gardener. For the next twenty years the Trust made few changes to the garden, although the Main Border was redesigned, using flowers and foliage of strong colours towards its east end grading to softer colours near the house.

The garden today

When restoration of Beningbrough began in 1977, the garden was also taken in hand. The two small formal gardens, which flank the house and are enclosed by yew hedges, were redesigned.

The Formal Gardens

That on the west side is in the style of a sixteenth-century knot garden, with low-growing plants in hot colours, laid out between dwarf box hedges; that on the east is planted in cool colours, predominantly pale blues, pinks and silvers, arranged around a rectangular pool with a central fountain. Versailles tubs filled with plants stand on York stone paving, which alternates with areas of cobbles. New garden seats have also been provided to a traditional pattern. The nearby variegated oak was planted by the Duke of Cambridge in 1898; its new leaves, which appear in August and September, are a delicate shade of pink. A sapling propagated from this oak was planted in January 1995 to commemorate the National Trust's centenary. The terrace terminates at its east end with an enormous Portugal Laurel. The plant has successfully layered itself and grown to a circumference of 73 metres. It is probably one of the largest laurels in the country.

The Adventure Playground

The small pleasure ground west of the house has been developed as an adventure playground, retaining its character as a wild garden with a circuit walk planted with evergreens and other ornamental plants.

The Double Border

A planting scheme for the Double Border next to the Walled Garden was devised in 1982 to extend the flowering season, which now begins in April with spring bulbs and ends in October with penstemons and nicotiana.

The Cherry Lawn Border

This large border was replanted in 1993–5 with contrasting foliage plants to create a subdued effect. The colour scheme ranges from hot shades at the eastern end to more pastel tones at the western.

Apples grown in the Walled Garden

Acklam Russet	Golden Harvey
Baumann's Reinette	Golden Noble
Blenheim Orange	Golden Russet
Bramley Seedling	Golden Spire
Broad Eyed Pippin	Gooseberry
Calville Blanc D'Hiver	Grenadier
Catshead	Hawthorndean
Charles Ross	Holland Pippin
Cockpit	Irish Peach
Court of Wick	Lemon Pippin
Cox's Orange Pippin	Margil
Duke of Devonshire	Orange Goff
Dumelow's Wellington	Ribston Pippin
Golden Reinette	Summer Golden Pippin
	Yorkshire Greening

The Walled Garden

The Walled Garden, initially maintained by the Trust as a grassed area for picnicking and events, was restored in 1995 thanks to generous donations. The original paths were re-created, and over 120 fruit trees were planted, using old varieties known to have been grown in the York area in the early nineteenth century. New borders, with box-edging, were provided for flowers, herbs and vegetables. Two double borders of lavender were planted at the west and east ends. A new planting scheme was also devised for the borders edging the original alley of espalier pears. Within the hollow walls a series of surviving pipes and flues, heated by

seventeen fires, once gave off sufficient heat to protect peaches and nectarines from frost.

Hebes, Choisya and Purple Vine thrive against the warm south-facing wall of the South Border, which is planted mainly with evergreen shrubs. It leads to the American Garden.

(Above) *The pear avenue in the Walled Garden*

(Below) *Lilies and yellow Mount Etna Broom fill a border on the north side of the house*

The American Garden

Beds of acid soil have been introduced to the naturally alkaline ground of the American Garden to support the collection of magnolias, azaleas and rhododendrons, many of which were introduced to Britain in the early nineteenth century.

The early Bourchiers

Ralph Bourchier and the Elizabethan house

The long Bourchier connection with Beningbrough began in 1556, when Ralph Bourchier inherited the estate on the death of his uncle, John Banester. Ralph Bourchier's father, James, was the illegitimate son of John Bourchier, 2nd Lord Berners, Chancellor of the Exchequer in 1516 and one of the Knights who attended Henry VIII at the Field of Cloth of Gold in 1520. However, Berners's most lasting achievement is his masterly translation of Froissart's *Chronicles*, published in 1523, the first into English of this famous history of the Hundred Years War. The Bourchiers had been one of the most illustrious and powerful of English noble families in the fourteenth and fifteenth centuries. Lord Berners numbered among his ancestors Thomas Bourchier of Knole, Archbishop of Canterbury, who officiated at the coronations of Edward IV, Richard III and Henry VII.

What did Elizabethan Beningbrough look like?

In the absence of any plans or records of its appearance, one can only surmise that it was a red-brick manor house on a modest scale, a house of the gentry rather than the nobility, with perhaps half a dozen main rooms, many of them panelled. The most tangible evidence of his occupation is the Elizabethan panelling which was later re-used to finish some of the second-floor rooms in the present house. One of the panels can be dated before 1577, the year when Ralph Bourchier remarried, for it is inlaid with the initials 'RBE', which link his name with that of his first wife, Elizabeth Hall.

Sir Ralph Bourchier, painted in 1582. He built the Elizabethan manor house which once stood near the site of the present house (private collection)

Ralph Bourchier built all or part of Elizabethan Beningbrough some 300 metres south-east of the present house. He was 25 when he inherited the estate in 1556. Bourchier had previously inherited estates in Staffordshire from his father and in 1571 was first elected to Parliament as MP for Newcastle-under-Lyme. It is not known exactly when he moved to Beningbrough, but between 1568 and 1575 he sold most of his land in Staffordshire and was certainly at Beningbrough by 1576.

In later life Ralph Bourchier rose to a place of some prominence in Yorkshire: he was High Sheriff in 1580–1, knighted in 1584, and an MP for the county in 1589. At his death, most of his property went not to his elder son, William, who was declared insane, but to one of his grandsons. The eldest of these, Robert, died unmarried at the age of eighteen in 1606, so it was to William's second son, John, that Beningbrough passed. Since he was then under age, the estate was put in the jurisdiction of the Court of Wards, an action which was later to have unfortunate consequences.

John Bourchier and the Civil War

This John Bourchier was born in about 1590 and knighted in 1619. Of the Beningbrough Bourchiers he is the only one to stand out above the run of worthy Yorkshire squires, for he played a prominent part in national events.

Sir John was an eccentric and highly irascible individual, determined to fight for his rights and beliefs whatever the consequences. A Puritan, he was described by a contemporary as 'a serious person, an open professor of religion'. His early career was overshadowed by battles with the Court of Wards over his estate. He was the most prominent of the few North Riding landowners who refused to pay the forced loan which Charles I levied in 1627 so as to avoid having to seek funds from Parliament.

Sir John's greatest foe was no less a person than Thomas Wentworth, the future Earl of Strafford and a fellow Yorkshireman. As President of the Council of the North from 1628, Strafford persuaded the King to agree to give up the centuries-old Royal Forest of Galtres and to create a thousand-acre deer-park. Sir John claimed that this enclosure infringed on common rights long held by the Bourchiers.

'A just act'

On 27 January 1649 Sir John was one of 49 judges who passed sentence of death on the King. At the Restoration he faced trial and execution like other regicides, but died in December 1660 while his case was still pending, asserting to the last the justice of the King's condemnation: 'I tell you it was a just act; God and all good men will own it.'

Sir John Bourchier, who owned Beningbrough in the first half of the seventeenth century (private collection)

He brought his complaint to the King's attention by deliberately pulling down the fences while Charles I was hunting in the park in the summer of 1633. Strafford wrote of the case, saying 'as concerning Sir John Bourchier and his insolent carriage, it is his daily bread, the man is little better than mad, one grain more would weigh him down to a direct Fury'. For his offence Sir John was heavily fined and imprisoned until October 1634. He never forgot this indignity. Seven years later, after Strafford's fall from power, Sir John was revenged when his case formed one of the lesser charges against Strafford, who was executed for treason.

In the Civil War, Sir John wholeheartedly supported the Parliamentary cause, organising the local militia and acting on the committee of the Northern Association for the defence of Yorkshire and adjoining counties. Through his mother, Katherine Barrington, he was related to Sir Thomas Barrington, the Parliamentary general, and to Oliver Cromwell himself.

The three Barrington Bourchiers

Sir John's son, Barrington Bourchier, was named after his grandmother's family, the Barringtons of Essex, staunch Puritans. There were to be three successive Barrington Bourchiers at Beningbrough between 1660 and 1700.

The first Barrington rescued the family estates from the threat of forfeiture. Like his father, he held a number of local offices during the Commonwealth, but he lacked his father's strongly Puritan spirit and decided to take up the cause of Charles II. He was persuaded to join in Sir George Booth's abortive insurrection against the Commonwealth in August 1659 'on assurance that his father's offence would be no prejudice to him if he would so assist'. In the disorder which followed Oliver Cromwell's death, General Monck marched south from Scotland to reinstate the Long Parliament and secure new elections. On his southward march he was met and welcomed to York by Barrington Bourchier, recently High Sheriff of the County, who was prominent among those who signed the Yorkshire declaration in support of a free Parliament in February 1660. As a result of his boldness, Barrington was deprived of office and apparently imprisoned, albeit only briefly. For when new elections were called in April 1660, he was chosen to sit as the MP for Thirsk. It was this Parliament, the first to be elected since 1640, which invited Charles II to return from exile.

At the following election Barrington did not stand, retiring from public life, safe in the knowledge that his estates were secure. These he considerably expanded during the 1660s, purchasing the adjacent manors of Overton and Shipton. At the same time he must have set about enlarging Beningbrough, for an increase from six to eleven hearths was recorded in the Hearth Tax Returns between 1662 and 1665.

Barrington's son, the second Barrington, was knighted by Charles II at Newmarket in 1676 at the age of 25. Like his father, he devoted his energies to local affairs and his own estates. In the tumultuous year of the Revolution in 1688, he was not alone in losing his position – he was Deputy Lieutenant of the North Riding – only to have it restored later the same year, when James II realised that his aims were not to be achieved by bullying. Sir Barrington died aged 44 in 1695. He was survived by his third wife and by five sons aged between two and 23. Three of those sons, Barrington, John and Ralph, were to come into the estate over the course of the next 65 years.

In April 1697, less than two years after his father's death, Barrington Bourchier, the third of this name, was knighted by William III at Kensington Palace. Little is known of his short tenure at Beningbrough but that he had ideas for improving the appearance of the estate. This is evident from his correspondence with the 'ingenious' Thomas Kirke of Leeds, whom Sir Barrington compliments on the 'delicate cutts and ridings' in his wood at Moseley, asking him 'to doe something of that nature' for Beningbrough.

This Sir Barrington married well. His wife, Mary Compton, was the daughter of Sir Francis Compton, Lieutenant-Colonel in the Horse Guards and a son of the 2nd Earl of Northampton. But tragedy followed: Barrington's first son was buried in 1699; Barrington's brother,

Beningbrough in 1695

An intriguing glimpse of Beningbrough before the house was rebuilt by John Bourchier comes from the inventory of Sir Barrington's personal estate at his death. Of the eighteen rooms in the house, the two most richly furnished were the Best Lodging with a blue damask bed, the contents being valued at the considerable figure of £45 5s, and the tapestry-hung Green Room with a bed upholstered in green and eight matching chairs. Much of the inventory is devoted to the kitchen quarters, stables and home farm. No less than £667 10s of the estate's total value of £1,413 was in ready money, kept in various bags and purses 'in the drawers: in Sr. Barrington's Chamber'.

Mark, died in December the same year, only to be swiftly followed by his wife and second son and by Sir Barrington himself some months later.

A young heir

Thus at the age of only sixteen, John Bourchier, Barrington's half-brother, came into the estate. He was the eldest surviving son of Sir Barrington senior and Margaret Hardwick. His mother had died in 1689, when he was but five, and his father in 1695. Though he was named as heir and sole executor in the will of his half-brother, Sir Barrington junior, he was too young to act and he 'spontaneously and voluntarily' chose his aunt, Elizabeth Clavering, 'for tutor and guardian'. No record survives of John's education, but we do know that at the age of 20 he set off to Italy on a Grand Tour which was to fill him full of ideas for a new house at Beningbrough.

Mary, Lady Bourchier, wife of the third Barrington Bourchier; attributed to William Wissing (Ferens Art Gallery, Hull)

The building of Beningbrough

Beningbrough is an enigma. It is one of the most remarkable Baroque houses in England, standing proud in the flat landscape, the façades a bright red brick ornamented with stone, the interiors richly carved and finished. But almost nothing is known of its building history.

What we do know of Beningbrough is that it was built for John Bourchier after his return from Italy and marriage to a wealthy Yorkshire heiress, that William Thornton, a talented carpenter-architect from York, was responsible at least for supervising the construction, and that the house was substantially complete by 1716.

Thomas Archer, one of the few British architects with first-hand knowledge of contemporary Baroque buildings in Rome, may have given advice on the more Italianate features of Beningbrough's design. But as we now know that John Bourchier visited Italy, it seems quite likely that he himself played a major part in the design. The early eighteenth century was a time when an interest in architecture was an acceptable accomplishment for a young man. Whatever the precise process at Beningbrough, the strong influence of recent Italian architecture on the form and decoration of the exterior of the house makes it clear that Bourchier's two-year tour of the Continent was of central importance in forming his taste.

An education in taste

It was probably in the summer of 1704 that the 20-year-old John Bourchier set out for Italy on the Grand Tour, an experience which by then was coming to be seen as an essential part of the education of a rich young man. By 1 September he had reached Padua where his name is to be found inscribed in the book of visitors to Padua University as 'John Bourchier of Yorkshire'. By 25 September Bourchier was in Rome, recorded as 'lately arrived from England' by the 1st Duke of Shrewsbury. The Duke, long resident in Rome, kept a constant watch for English visitors, as his journals reveal. On 9 November he notes: 'All the English gentlemen in town dined with me. We were 14 at table.' This presumably included Bourchier, who called on the Duke again in December and on 21 April the following year, 1705. If Bourchier needed a mentor in this city of riches, he could not have found a more knowledgeable fellow-countryman than the Duke, who had gone out of his way to study the Baroque churches and palaces of Rome. The Duke is known to have been in touch with the prolific publishing family, De Rossi, and may therefore have been responsible for showing Bourchier Domenico de Rossi's newly published *Studio d'Architettura Civile*, a volume which appears to have been an important influence on the appearance of Beningbrough. Bourchier was still in Rome

Thomas Patch's caricature shows English gentlemen enjoying the pleasures of Italy. John Bourchier must have been entertained in much the same way by the Duke of Shrewsbury when he stayed in Rome

The marquetry roundel on the Great Staircase bears the initials of John and Mary Bourchier and the date 1716, when their new house was probably almost complete

towards the end of the year, and seems to have been well provided for, if we can judge from a letter sent home by another young Yorkshireman, Viscount Irwin of Temple Newsam. Writing from Rome on 5 December 1705, Lord Irwin complains of the meagreness of his funds, regretting how he is 'much inferior in everything than Mr Boucher, who has tho' but a gentleman, a greater allowance than I'.

Bourchier probably returned home in 1706. Two years later at the age of 24 he married Mary Bellwood at Acomb parish church in York. It was 'the long expected match' of 'a dapper couple', according to Anne Clavering, Bourchier's childhood friend (she was his guardian's stepdaughter). A year older than her husband, Mary had, like him, been left an orphan, at the age of eleven on the death of her father, Roger Bellwood, Sergeant-at-Law in York and London. It was perhaps the marriage settlement which provided John Bourchier with the security to embark on the expensive task of building a new house.

Building Beningbrough

At Beningbrough the site chosen was a very slight rise above the general level of the Ouse flood plain, not far from the Elizabethan manor. This would probably have remained the home of John and Mary Bourchier and their two young children while the new house was being built. The speed of construction would have depended on the scale of Bourchier's resources, but, judging from the pace of work on contemporary houses, building and fitting out may well have taken five or six years. This would imply that Beningbrough was begun in 1710 or 1711. By May 1714 – the earliest documented mention of the new house – the building was well enough advanced for the glazing of the windows to be all or part complete. The house was presumably substantially finished and fitting out well advanced by 1716, the date on the elaborate marquetry roundel on the half-landing of the Great Staircase. In the Saloon there was once a pair of overdoors by Jacob Bogdani dated 1720, suggesting that the furnishing of the house may have taken a number of years to complete.

William Thornton

William Thornton, the supervising architect at Beningbrough, was born in about 1670 and trained as a carpenter and joiner. His name is linked to the Bourchiers and so to Beningbrough by two eighteenth-century sources, a list of Yorkshire houses within a copy of *The Builder's Dictionary* of 1734 in the Metropolitan Museum, New York, where he is described as architect of 'Mr Bourchier's', and letters from him to the agent of a later Earl of Strafford. Writing on 5 May 1714 about his work at Wentworth Castle, he recommends glazing bars of 'ye same thickness I have done for Mr Bourchier & others'. In August the same year he mentions having 'wainscotted most of ye rooms at ... Mr Bourchiers'. The monument erected in St Olave's church in York at Thornton's death in 1721 refers to him specifically as 'Joyner and Architect'. As joiner he is known to have worked on the fitting out of several Yorkshire houses during the first two decades of the eighteenth century. He also had some practice as an architect, like a number of talented craftsmen of the York school ('Workmen advanc'd to the degree of Architects' as Hawksmoor patronisingly put it). He restored the north transept of Beverley Minster in 1716–20 but, apart from his work at Beningbrough, his only other recorded commissions as an architect are for minor buildings at Swinton Park and Ledston Hall, both in Yorkshire.

Baroque formality

In the formality of its planning, Beningbrough bears resemblance to a number of other grand Baroque houses of the period. The house is laid out on strong cross-axes, with central doorways on the north and south fronts opposing each other and transverse corridors running the length of the house from east to west on the two principal floors. Beningbrough has a monumental entrance hall on the north front rising through two storeys and a line of state rooms along the garden front which faces south. This is the pattern promoted by Vanbrugh and which Thornton would have seen at Castle Howard, where he worked between 1708 and 1711.

Externally, the compact rectangle of the house is plain and lacks a grand portico or pediment. The use of red brick with architectural details in stone is firmly in the English tradition and would have been less expensive than building entirely in stone as at Castle Howard or Bramham. The chief material used for Beningbrough is a hard crusted brick, made locally from the different coloured alluvial clay beds along the banks of the Ouse. The finely pointed principal fronts are a combination of red and orange, while the screen walls and pavilions flanking the forecourt are in another kind of brick, paler, less carefully graded in size, and laid with rough mortar – suggesting that they were built a few years either before or after the main block. The bricks are of exceptionally small size, about 23 by 5 cm.

In a rather old-fashioned way the main façades consist of two equal storeys raised on a low basement. But for all its apparent simplicity the exterior has several unconventional features which are very obviously derived from Italian sources, and in particular the engravings of Roman palaces to be found in a number of recently published volumes. It is here that John Bourchier's contribution to the design is likely to have been most pronounced. The use of massive console brackets to support an overhanging cornice, even down to the idea of inset windows, is found at the Palazzo Altieri, illustrated in Ferrerio and Falda's *Palazzi di Roma*.

Another idea which can be traced to Ferrerio and Falda's volume is the choice of alternately raised and recessed strips of dressed stone – an unusual form of quoining – to mark the slight projections in Beningbrough's façades; on the garden front these quoins are restricted to the end bays as on Borromini's College of the Sapienza at Rome. The curious window frame above the entrance door, with curved ears and a central fluted triglyph as a keystone, comes from Bernini's Palazzo Chigi in Rome, reproduced in the first volume of Domenico de Rossi's *Studio d'Architettura Civile*, published in 1702. Similar window frames are found at Heythrop in Oxfordshire, the house begun in 1707 by Thomas Archer for the Duke of Shrewsbury, whom Bourchier had of course met in Rome. The pairs of massive scaled wooden console brackets supporting the frieze at Beningbrough, terminating in dentils of the Doric order, are also paralleled at Heythrop House (and at St Paul's, Deptford, designed by Archer in 1712), although they may be based on one of 'Trois diferents Corniches' engraved by Daniel Marot in his *Nouveau Livre d'Ornements* (of about 1700) rather than on an Italian source.

The south front

The central window on the north front, with its curious ear-like projections, is based on an engraving of Bernini's Palazzo Chigi in Rome

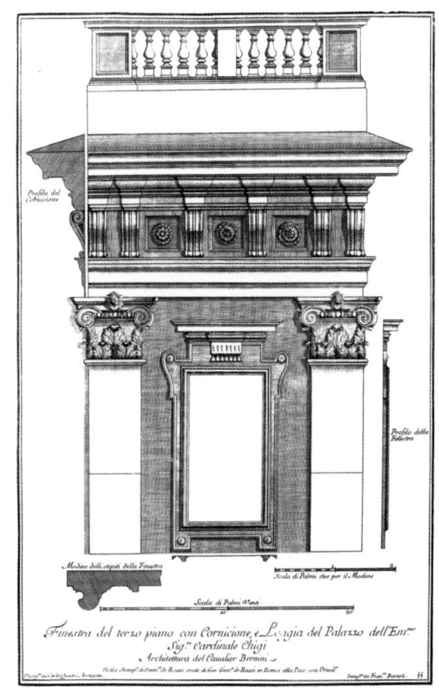

Archer, as an amateur gentleman-architect, may have given advice to John Bourchier on various points of detail, while Thornton acted as executant architect-cum-builder.

Once the house had been roofed and the windows glazed, attention would have turned to the fitting out of the interior. Again there was some attempt to save expense, for the Hall is painted plaster above a plinth of stone rather than stone throughout, as in some grander Yorkshire houses. It is in the profusion of superb woodwork and carving in the state rooms leading off the Hall that the interiors are at their richest. The carving is as remarkable in its way as Samuel Watson's at Chatsworth or John Seldon's at Petworth, approaching at times the assurance of Grinling Gibbons himself. Thoresby, writing in 1702, refers to work which 'the most celebrated Gibbons wrought at York' with the mason-architect John Etty, and the skill shown by the York school of carvers here may therefore derive from first-hand contact with the greatest craftsman of the day.

The finely carved overdoors were the work of William Thornton's team of craftsmen

The only early painted view of Beningbrough, dated 1751, shows large pedimented service blocks facing each other across the forecourt. Were they ever built? It has been suggested that this painting is no more than a record of a scheme for proposed additions. But if so, why are the two blocks shown with mullion-and-transom windows which were quite out of fashion by the mid-eighteenth century? It seems more likely that John Bourchier had these rather unadventurous service quarters built at the same time or very soon after the main house, and that they were pulled down when the existing stable block was built in the late eighteenth century.

The craftsmen of Beningbrough

Although no accounts survive for Beningbrough, we know the names of a few highly skilled craftsmen who worked with Thornton elsewhere. At Wentworth Castle his chief assistant (and later his successor) was a French Huguenot craftsman, the wood-carver Jonathan Godier (anglicised to Goodyear). It is easy to point to small similarities in the two houses – for example, the paired cornice brackets in the Drawing Room are found at Wentworth, as are the lambrequins or draped plinths which ornament the overdoors. Thornton also regularly worked with another Huguenot, the stone- and wood-carver Daniel Hervé

The Bourchier coat of arms may have been carved by Daniel Hervé

(or Harvey), who may perhaps have carved the great stone coat of arms over the garden door to the house. During the early eighteenth century there was a flourishing school of Huguenot craftsmen at work in the North, many of them exiled from France as Protestants following the Revocation of the Edict of Nantes in 1685. Given Thornton's close association with such craftsmen, it is not surprising to find that the dominant influence at work in the panelled rooms at Beningbrough is French. Many features of the wood-carving have their origins in recent French publications, and in particular the engraved work of Jean Bérain and his pupil, the Huguenot Daniel Marot (see p. 21). However, it was probably only the carvers at Beningbrough who were French. The magnificent wrought-iron grilles in the Hall have been attributed stylistically to the famous Derbyshire blacksmith Robert Bakewell. Another craftsman linked with Thornton, and so probably with Beningbrough, is the York plasterer John Bagnall, who worked at Castle Howard and at Hotham's house at Beverley, and who was to be one of Thornton's executors in 1721.

Rather plainer in style than the house are the two small flanking pavilions built of brown brick. These buildings cannot be much later in date than the house itself, for they are to be seen in Samuel Buck's drawing of Beningbrough made between 1719 and 1723 (reproduced on p. 39).

Later life

Of John Bourchier's later life remarkably little is known. He was High Sheriff of Yorkshire in 1720 as his grandfather had been before him and his son was to be after. He took an interest in the York races, subscribing to the stake money, and he also subscribed £25 in 1730 to a venture of particular importance in York's eighteenth-century history, the building of the Assembly Rooms. John Bourchier died in 1736 at the age of 52, leaving one of the grandest new houses in Yorkshire as his monument.

He was followed at Beningbrough by his son, also John, who in 1738 married an heiress, Mildred Roundell, in York Minster. This John Bourchier and his wife feature prominently in York society. He was High Sheriff in 1749 and he built one of the finest town houses in York, Micklegate House, completed in 1752. At that time the city was the main focus for cultural life in the north of England, and various county families preferred to make York rather than London their home when not staying on their estates. In the summer the Bourchiers would sometimes be found staying in Bristol or taking the waters at Bath. And it was at Bath that John Bourchier died in 1759, aged 49. Sadly his only child, Mildred, died the following year within months of her marriage to Robert Fox Lane, the son of the MP for York.

Micklegate House became the home of John Bourchier's widow, while Beningbrough was claimed by his uncle, Dr Ralph Bourchier, then aged 71, a successful physician who had made London his home. He agreed to pass his interest in the house and the 7,000-acre estate to his only daughter, Margaret Bourchier, who was to live at Beningbrough for the next seven decades.

John Bourchier the younger; by John Vanderbank, 1732. Bourchier lived at Beningbrough in the mid-eighteenth century and built Micklegate House in York

The later owners of Beningbrough

The Earles

Of all the owners of Beningbrough, it was Margaret Bourchier, the last of her line, who held the house for longest, over 65 years in all. She married Giles Earle at Hendon in Middlesex in 1761, when the *York Courant* described her as 'an Heiress with a very great fortune'.

The Earles were an unconventional couple. One acquaintance called her 'this curious woman ... such a complete Gig [flighty girl] that I was quite entertained with her'. Her husband was the son of a Whig MP, but, unlike his father or grandfather before him, he took little part in public life. A French visitor to Beningbrough in 1768 acknowledged him as 'a good judge of character, with an exquisite sense, of free and strong opinions', but noted his pessimistic view of his fellow beings and his boastfulness about himself.

Probably the year after this visit Beningbrough was shut up and the family left for the Continent. What led the Earles, by then both in their thirties and with one child, to venture abroad for several years is not known. It seems that they made a lengthy stay in Paris before going on to Italy. The Earles were in Rome by November 1770 where they met Dr Charles Burney, the historian of music, and they spent much of the summer of 1771 at Cardinal Albani's villa at Castel Gandolfo, close to the Pope's summer palace. In December that year the antiquary James Byres wrote to Sir William Hamilton, British envoy at Naples, reporting their departure, adding his opinion of the Earles: 'They are, I really think, good natured well meaning people, and had they not lived at Paris some time would have done very well.' Their Italian souvenirs included a bust of the Pope, Clement XIV, by Christopher Hewetson, which still sits on the Hall chimneypiece at Beningbrough, a set of views of Naples and Vesuvius by Pietro Antoniani, dated 1771, and a marble vase supplied by Piranesi, who dedicated to them three plates in his series of etchings, *Vasi, Candelabri, Cippi ...*, first published as a collection in 1778.

That Margaret Earle came back home with continental airs emerges from an amusing letter written by Theresa Parker of Saltram to her brother, Frederick Robinson of Newby Park, in 1774. Mrs Earle is described as being 'dressed very French' and speaking in 'as broken English as if she had never seen England for more than two months'. Her manner 'is so far improved that as before you could only be amused with her absurdities, she is kind enough to carry them

(Left) Mrs Margaret Earle, the last of the Bourchier line; by Sir William Beechey (private collection)

Giles Earle in old age (private collection)

to the highest degree'. At Beningbrough the Earles appear to have experienced a financial crisis. The estate was mortgaged for £12,000 in 1777, and in the following year one correspondent wrote of Giles Earle's precipitate departure for Calais, having paid off all his servants. It was probably only after the sale of Hendon House in 1785 that the Earles' financial situation eased, and what few improvements they made at Beningbrough, such as the stables and the new lodge at Newton, probably belong to the period of their greater prosperity.

'If you wish to see Mrs E. in all her glory, you must look in at the ball this night', wrote Giles Earle in 1805 to his solicitor, Joseph Munby at York, who was evidently something of a friend as well as a man of business. These few surviving letters written between 1802 and 1806 provide a rare glimpse of Giles Earle's character in old age. He deemed money well laid out if 'the result shall be neatness or convenience in the roads or grounds contiguous to or leading to Beningbrough Hall'. But he complained of his tenants' requests for farm improvements: 'I dare indeed hardly venture out my house, being way-laid ... by numerous petitioners for petty favours who covet my posts & rails and timber, and would equally covet my ox & my ass, if I had any.' As time went on, it was his own well-being which was his abiding concern: 'My health hangs, like a Mahomet's coffin, between heaven and earth, with a preponderancy rather to earth but I hope to escape both being on the turf and under it this year.'

Giles Earle did not die until 1811 at the age of 78. His two sons had predeceased him, fighting in the war against Napoleon. Who was to inherit Beningbrough? Mrs Earle's choice fell on the Rev. William Henry Dawnay, the future 6th Viscount Downe, and when his first son was born in 1812, she acted as godparent. Not only were the Dawnays distantly related to the Bourchiers by marriage, but William Henry Dawnay had been a close friend of her elder son at Eton.

Margaret Earle died at Beningbrough in October 1827 at the age of 87. To use the words of the epitaph added to her husband's monument in Hendon church, 'Mrs Earle was the last of one of the most ancient families in England; the Bourchiers having their origin from the remotest period of antiquity.'

(Right) The stables were built by the Earles, probably after 1785

The Dawnays

From 1827 to 1916 Beningbrough was owned by the Dawnays, an old Yorkshire family with a strong tradition of service in Parliament, the Church and the Army. The principal Dawnay residence was Cowick Hall in the West Riding and later Wykeham Abbey near Scarborough. Remarkably few alterations were made to Beningbrough until the 1890s, perhaps because the house was used as a secondary residence, usually occupied by a younger son of the family.

William Henry Dawnay, the heir to the Beningbrough estate, was the second son of John Dawnay, 4th Viscount Downe, a Whig MP for 20 years. Like many a younger son Dawnay went into the Church, becoming Rector of two family livings in Yorkshire in 1796. At the age of 55 he inherited Beningbrough and five years later in 1832 he became 6th Viscount at the death of his elder brother.

Lord Downe resigned his church livings and moved to Beningbrough with his wife, Lydia. They made various improvements to the house and grounds in the 1830s. It was probably at this time that a gallery was installed over the Hall to improve circulation at first-floor level, and two ground-floor rooms amalgamated to form a decent-sized drawing-room of the sort which had by then become necessary for entertaining. Lord Downe died at Beningbrough in 1846, worth £80,000, and his widow followed him two years later. The Beningbrough estate was inherited by their younger son, Payan Dawnay, and his sister, another Lydia, who together shared Beningbrough for more than 40 years. Little happened to the house in their time, for brother and sister lived quietly, devoting themselves to public-spirited activities and the welfare of their tenants.

The Dawnays of this generation were great church builders. The 6th Viscount rebuilt Newton church in 1839. His eldest son, the 7th Viscount, made a vow to build three new churches when he married Mary Bagot, the daughter of the Bishop of Bath and Wells, in 1843. He was an early patron of the High Victorian architect William Butterfield, commissioning from him a series of churches in Yorkshire and Rutland, and some remarkable estate housing. His brother and sister at Beningbrough, Payan and Lydia, followed his example,

(Right) Lydia Dawnay; by F. R. Say, 1854 (private collection). She inherited Beningbrough from her father, the 6th Viscount Dawnay, in 1846, and lived here with her brother Payan for the next 44 years

rebuilding three local churches – Shipton, Newton (again) and Overton – between 1848 and 1855, to the designs of the Yorkshire railway station architect G. T. Andrews. They also built and maintained two local schools, and modernised cottages and tenant farms on the estate.

Lydia Dawnay died aged 76 in January 1890 and her brother, Payan, aged 75 in June the following year. The estate was inherited by their nephew, Lieutenant-Colonel Lewis Payn Dawnay, the second of the six surviving sons of the 7th Viscount. With his coming, Beningbrough was transformed. For the first time in more than a century the house and gardens reverberated to the sound of a young family: skating on the pond in winter and cricket weeks in summer, amateur theatricals in the Hall, battledore and shuttlecock in the gallery, 'tobogganing' down the main staircase, house parties and entertainments.

Lady Victoria Grey, who married Colonel Lewis Dawnay in 1877. They settled at Beningbrough in 1892 and spent large sums modernising the house

In 1877 Lewis Dawnay had married Victoria Grey, granddaughter of Lord Grey, the Prime Minister. Soon afterwards he resigned his commission in the Coldstream Guards and in 1880 was elected to Parliament for the Thirsk Division, which he continued to represent until 1892. At the time of inheriting Beningbrough, he and his wife and four young children were living at Bookham Grove, near Dorking, Surrey, a property which had long been in the Dawnay family. For a time Beningbrough was let, but in August 1892 the Dawnays moved in, making it their main home. Over the next two decades rather more than £18,000 was spent on improving the house and its surroundings. Electricity was installed and every farm on the estate (about 45 in all) was modernised at a total cost of £13,500. The Conservatory and a new service wing, subsequently demolished, were added in 1892 at a cost of £7,725 under the direction of the architect Colonel R. W. Edis, known for his work in the Queen Anne style. The forecourt was remodelled the following year, when the iron gates were hung by Starkie Gardner at a cost of £119.

The house became a centre of political as well as social activity, for Colonel Dawnay continued to campaign actively for the Conservatives after he had ceased to be a local MP. The Colonel was a man of firm convictions and strong temper. 'He was a very impatient and restless man, known in the family as "The Fidgets" ', according to his grandson, Christopher Dawnay. At his death in 1910, the *Yorkshire Evening Press* obituary called him 'somewhat brusque and abrupt in manner ... He was extremely outspoken and not overgiven to mincing words; so his political and other opponents might reckon on getting it straight from the shoulder.'

Guy Dawnay

Colonel Dawnay left two sons and two daughters. The elder son, Major-General Guy Payan Dawnay, had fought in South Africa during the Boer War and in 1906 he married Cecile Buxton. When Guy Dawnay inherited Beningbrough in 1910 at the age of 32, he made good his earlier intention and left the Army to take up a career in merchant banking. In his diaries he emerges as a more thoughtful man than his father, an innovator and reformer during his Army days, a Liberal with a commitment to the 'public services' and a businessman professing no feeling for money for its own sake. He was also an early supporter of the National Trust through his friendship with Nigel Bond, its then Secretary, and pledged his support for the Trust's first country house appeal in 1906, when Barrington Court in Somerset was at risk.

At the outbreak of war in 1914 Guy Dawnay was recalled to the Army, eventually joining the British Expeditionary Force to Palestine which led to the capture of Jerusalem in 1917. Dawnay was Deputy Chief of Staff to General Allenby and a brilliant intelligence officer, playing a leading role as strategist for the Palestine campaign.

In June 1916 Dawnay was in England on leave, probably at Beningbrough where his wife spent much of the summer, and it was then that they decided to sell the house. The sale took place in his absence later that year. For a time there were rumours that the house would be pulled down. Perhaps for this reason Dawnay suggested to his wife in January 1917 that the Government should take it over to let as flats to impoverished war widows or disabled officers: 'There must be so many who would love to live cheaply in beautiful surroundings ... and if it were possible one would not feel the waste of that beautiful house.'

Why did Guy Dawnay sell Beningbrough? Apart from needing the money – the duty on his father's estate was not finally paid off until after the sale – his chosen career as a merchant banker meant that he had to be near London. He did not wish to be an absentee landlord and his wife seems not to have liked Beningbrough. After the war he bought Longparish House in Hampshire and returned to business, becoming chairman of a number of leading companies and starting his own merchant bank, Dawnay Day.

The Beningbrough sale took place at the Festival Concert Rooms, York, in November 1916. The estate of 6,100 acres was broken up by the purchaser, a Cambridgeshire farmer and speculator, William Abel Towler. It had cost him only £137,000, a price which reflected the years of agricultural depression. The Hall, Home Farm and Park, some 375 acres in all, were later sold on privately to Lady Chesterfield for the very low sum of £15,000. With her husband, Lord Chesterfield, she took possession of the house in July 1917. Thus Beningbrough entered an Indian summer at a time when the country house was coming under increasing threat.

Guy Dawnay described by T. E. Lawrence in *The Seven Pillars of Wisdom*:

Dawnay was mainly intellect ... Dawnay's cold, shy mind gazed upon our efforts with bleak eye, always thinking, thinking. Beneath this mathematical surface he hid passionate, many-sided convictions, a reasoned scholarship in higher warfare, and the brilliant bitterness of a judgement disappointed with us, and with life.
He was the least professional of soldiers, a banker who read Greek History, a strategist unashamed, and a burning poet with strength over daily things.

The Hall in 1906, when a gallery connected the first-floor corridors

Lady Chesterfield

Lady Chesterfield was born Enid Edith Wilson, the fourth of seven children of a wealthy shipowner, Charles Wilson of Hull, and his wife Florence Wellesley, a great-niece of the 1st Duke of Wellington. A Liberal MP for many years, Wilson had built up the Wilson Line into the largest privately owned shipping company in the world; he was created 1st Baron Nunburnholme in 1906, the year before his death.

Wilson's four daughters were wealthy heiresses, and their mother was determined that they should marry well. In 1900 at the age of 21, Enid married Edwyn Francis Scudamore-Stanhope, 10th Earl of Chesterfield, an eligible bachelor rather more than twice her age. He was a Privy Counsellor who had held posts in the Royal Household, and a Liberal like her father. He had probably first met his future bride five years earlier when he acted as best man at the wedding of her elder sister. The Chesterfields lived at Holme Lacy in Herefordshire until 1909 when Lord Chesterfield sold his ancestral home for nearly £200,000 and moved to London.

The Chesterfields furnished Beningbrough in great style with pictures, furniture and Gibbons carvings from Holme Lacy, as can be seen in the *Country Life* articles on the house in 1927. By this time much had been done to adapt Beningbrough to their tastes. In the Hall the gallery was removed and the pilasters marbled. The Dining Room was walnut-grained and the architectural details picked out in gold, while in the State Bedchamber and the Drawing Room the panelling was stripped, after the fashion of the day, to reveal the pinewood. A lift was installed in the back staircase and the Saloon painted a strident peacock blue. It is not known who was in charge of the work, but John Cornforth has suggested that it was strongly influenced by Lenygon & Morant, the architectural decorators who pioneered the renewal of interest in early English interiors. Morant & Co. restored the State Apartment bed, when it was still at Holme Lacy, and the labels of the merged firm have been found on the bed in Lady Chesterfield's Bedroom.

Lord Chesterfield was 68 in 1922 when he retired from his court appointment as Master of the Horse to George V. He seems to have spent much of his time in London apart from his wife, and their marriage was childless. When he died in 1933, the title passed to his brother only to become extinct some years later.

Lady Chesterfield's enduring interest was the stud farm which she had set up at Beningbrough in the early 1920s. It was her mother Lady

(Right) Enid, Countess of Chesterfield; by Ellis Roberts, 1900. The Chesterfields bought Beningbrough and furnished it lavishly with furniture and pictures from Holme Lacy

Edwyn, 10th Earl of Chesterfield; by F. E. Bertier

Nunburnholme's interest in racing which led her to change from breeding hunters to thoroughbreds, building up the stud to nine or ten brood mares. The most distinguished foal was Sun Castle, a black colt which Lady Chesterfield had the pleasure of leading in after it won the St Leger in 1941. This was her finest hour.

A wartime oasis

During the Second World War Beningbrough was requisitioned for use by airmen stationed at the RAF base at Linton-on-Ouse, 2½ miles away. The best of the furniture and pictures were locked up and Lady Chesterfield moved out to the Home Farm. Of the bomber squadrons based at Linton, the most famous was 76 Squadron under Wing-Commander Leonard Cheshire VC, who had just completed his book, *Bomber Pilot*, and was already a legendary figure. From time to time Cheshire would visit Beningbrough to see that all was well – and to listen to Lady Chesterfield's complaints about airmen trampling her vegetable garden.

For the men who slept on the top two floors and used the ground floor as a mess, Beningbrough was an oasis of peace. Sergeant Clifford Hill, a gunner in one of the seven-man crews of the great four-engined Halifax bombers based at Linton-on-Ouse, has left his reminiscences of his time at Beningbrough in 1943. Losses were heavy with almost nightly raids over Germany as far afield as Munich. But a safe return brought another world. 'After de-briefing and breakfast the seven of us would cycle in the early morning to a dawn chorus along country lanes to Beningbrough.' Later in 1943 Linton became home to two squadrons of the Royal Canadian Air Force, 426 'Thunderbird' Squadron and 408 'Flying Goose' Squadron.

Moving back in

After the war it took some time for the York firm of Walter Brierley to put the house in good repair, but in 1947 Lady Chesterfield, now aged 69, moved back into her old quarters. Many of those who worked on the estate or knew the house have left their own account of her character. Miss Constance Seabrook, the lady's maid who had to dress her three times on hunting days, recalls her demanding standards: 'I never had a hunting lady before, I nearly packed it in, then she seemed a bit kinder and I settled down and mastered her frantic ways.' Those of her former servants who have recorded their memories agree that, though eccentric in her ways, she was a fair and kind employer.

Lady Chesterfield died at Beningbrough in November 1957 at the age of 79. Though she had expressed a wish that Beningbrough should remain in the family, she seems to have understood that this was unlikely to be possible. There were death duties to pay and, as with so many estates in this post-war period, very little in the way of ready assets to meet liabilities. So her executors decided to offer the house to the Treasury.

The restoration of Beningbrough

Beningbrough came to the National Trust in June 1958. The house and estate had been accepted by the government in lieu of death duties at a cost of £29,250, using the National Land Fund (the forerunner of the National Heritage Memorial Fund). The 1950s were a time when land prices were still depressed, and in retrospect the period has come to be seen as a low point in the fortunes of the country house. It was a decade when numerous great estates were sold, the houses demolished or converted into schools or hospitals, and their contents dispersed. It was also the decade when the National Trust took on more great houses than at any other time in its history – some three or four a year.

When Beningbrough came to the Trust it was almost devoid of contents. In a great four-day sale held some months after Lady Chesterfield's death, those contents not retained by the family were dispersed at auction. Given the limited funds available and the widespread feeling then held that the Chesterfield furnishings, as relatively recent introductions, had no special association with the history of the house, the Trust's objectives at the auction had to be strictly limited. They were, as Robin Fedden, the Trust's Historic Buildings Secretary, recorded after the sale, 'to obtain those essential furnishings which might not make it impossible to let the house to a tenant and which would also provide an essential background to any furniture of our own which we might be able to put in – in other words, carpets, curtains, chandeliers, grates'. In these circumscribed aims the Trust was most successful, managing also to buy the few family portraits in the sale, the great state bed from Holme Lacy and the fine marquetry pier-tables and glasses in the Drawing Room. The Trust's Honorary Representative in Yorkshire, George Howard of Castle Howard, wrote to Robin Fedden: 'the gossip ... was that the only people who were bidding for these objects were ourselves and the Wills for Ditchley.' The 1950s were a period when fine things could still be obtained at country-house sales cheaply. The total cost of nearly £10,000 came from the National Land Fund.

BENINGBROUGH HALL

YORK

Situate about 8 miles from the City on the York to the West of the A.19 Road and 2½ miles due West of the Village of Shipton

THE

IMPORTANT

Contents of the Mansion

comprising

CHARLES II, JAMES II, WILLIAM & MARY, QUEEN ANNE AND EARLY GEORGIAN FURNITURE

including

A State Bed; Tallboy Chests; Wardrobes; Mirrors; Court Cupboard; Chests of Drawers; Dressing, Dining, Writing and Occasional Tables; Carved and Giltwood Console Tables; A Carlton House Table

A CHIPPENDALE MAHOGANY BOOKCASE, A BUREAU, A BREAKFAST TABLE and A SERPENTINE SHAPED FRONT CHEST

Sheraton Mahogany Sideboards; Six Hepplewhite Mahogany Fauteuil; French Writing Tables and Chairs; Italian and Lacquer Cabinets; Grandfather and other Clocks; Basket Grates; Torchères; Settees

PERSIAN, AUBUSSON, TURKEY AND ENGLISH CARPETS AND RUGS

17th CENTURY BRUSSELS TAPESTRY PANELS; NEEDLEWORK SCREENS

An Important Modern Giltwood Salon Suite; Easy Chairs and Stools; Carved Wood and Cut Glass Chandeliers and Wall Appliqué; Armoires; Pictures of the English and Dutch Schools, Engravings; Books; Old English and Chinese Porcelain and Cut Glass; Bijouterie; Linen

A COLLECTION OF OLD ENGLISH SILVER AND SHEFFIELD PLATE

and miscellaneous effects

which will be sold UPON THE PREMISES by

CURTIS & HENSON

5, Mount Street, Grosvenor Square, London, W.1

21, Horsefair, Banbury, Oxon

Telephone: GROsvenor 5131 (London); Banbury 3295

On TUESDAY, 10th JUNE, 1958, and THREE FOLLOWING DAYS commencing at 11 a.m. precisely each day

On View: WEDNESDAY, THURSDAY, and FRIDAY, 4th, 5th, and 6th JUNE, 1958
Between the hours of 9.30 a.m. and 4 p.m.

CATALOGUES (price 3/-) may be obtained from the Auctioneers, as above.

The Trust's early years at Beningbrough were not easy ones. Derelict outbuildings in the Laundry courtyard had to be demolished. The house, sparsely furnished as it was, presented a rather melancholy spectacle despite a certain grandeur. A curator was installed in 1961 when the house was first opened to the public but this arrangement was terminated in 1967, principally as a result of the difficulties of making opening pay its way on this basis. In 1968 the house was let to a tenant with the obligation to open to the public a number of afternoons a week, but this arrangement, though it brought more income, did not prove a satisfactory way of showing such a grand house. Visitors declined to no more than 2,000 a year and there were problems with the opening arrangements. By the mid-1970s the feeling was widespread that a new approach was needed. 'Dowdy and shabby' and 'a disgrace to the National Trust' are descriptions which were used.

The Holme Lacy state bed was bought at the Beningbrough sale

There was a further problem: finance. Beningbrough was the second of six major houses accepted by the National Trust from the government between 1957 and 1977 without any endowment to cover running costs. The understanding was that the annual shortfall would be made good through the agency of the Historic Buildings Council. On acquisition the annual costs were estimated at £2,430 and the income at £630. By 1976 the deficit had risen to £30,000 a year. So when a plan was proposed to improve the appearance of the house, attract more visitors and reduce the deficit, the idea was widely welcomed.

Transforming a 'cinderella'

The house was to be put into a good state of repair, the interiors restored and more fully furnished, the gardens replanted and a range of visitor facilities added in the outbuildings. The property was close to York with its many visitors and not far from the great urban centres of Leeds and Bradford. The aim was no less than to transform this 'cinderella' of Trust properties into a major tourist attraction. In the event, the whole process was to take almost four years from conception to completion.

One of the very first problems to be faced was the dearth of contents. Here the National Portrait Gallery came to the Trust's rescue. In June 1975 the Trust's Historic Buildings Secretary, St John Gore, approached Dr John Hayes, the Gallery's Director, for a substantial loan of late seventeenth- and early eighteenth-century portraits, which were shown throughout the house, with a special display on the second floor. Important as the pictures were, the Trust also had to rely extensively on bequests and gifts of furniture. Some of the outstanding walnut furniture at Beningbrough was left to the Trust by the late Lady Megaw in 1974, and a collection of oriental porcelain was given in 1975 by Miss Dorothy Bushell. More recent loans of ceramics, from the Ashmolean and Victoria & Albert museums, have also enriched the interior of the house.

Work begins

It was not until January 1976 that detailed planning could begin. By February 1977 all the preliminaries were complete, and Martin Stancliffe was appointed architect. Over the next two years, the roof leadwork was completely renewed, the top floor strengthened and dry rot at first-floor level eradicated. Then new services and security systems were fitted throughout with great care so that they did not impinge on the appearance of the building.

When it came to the redecoration of the interiors, the initial plan was to employ John Fowler, who had worked extensively for the Trust elsewhere. Following his visit to Beningbrough in November 1976, Lady Chesterfield's Dressing Room was redecorated, but sadly Fowler was forced to withdraw from further work shortly before his death in 1977. He was succeeded by David Mlinaric, who had begun working seriously on the decoration of country houses and historic interiors a few years before. Since Beningbrough, Mlinaric has gone on to supervise a whole series of important schemes, including Spencer House in London.

Work began with the Hall. In Lady Chesterfield's time the pilasters and the fireplace had been marbled and many other features painted or enriched. However, investigations in 1977 revealed that the plinths to the main pilasters were originally of simple dressed cream-coloured limestone; above that level all decoration had been carried out in plasterwork, probably painted in stone and off-white, in the manner of many other great halls of the period. The plinths and the chimneypiece were stripped of later layers of paint and used to provide the key to the rest of the colour scheme. At the same time the oak floor, a discordant later insertion, was removed for reuse in the restaurant and replaced by stone flags in two colours chosen to match those already in the staircase hall. The overall result was to emphasise the architectural qualities of the space.

What is now seen at Beningbrough is very much an attempt to re-create the spirit of the house rather than a restoration of its precise appearance at the time it was built. However, research into the original paint colours, begun in August 1977 by Ian Bristow, proved of some help in those rooms which had not been stripped to the bare pine earlier in the twentieth century. Examination of cross-sections of the layers of paintwork in the Hall, Dining Room,

(Right) The Hall and the corridors were painted in shades of white

Great Staircase and Saloon revealed extensive use of shades of white, off-white and pale-grey, typical of early eighteenth-century interiors.

For practical and aesthetic reasons, the decision was taken to reopen the doorway from the Dining Room into the State Bedchamber. Not only did this make it possible for visitors to make a circuit through the main rooms, it also restored the magnificent original enfilade view along the length of the rooms on the south front, importan for understanding the layout of a Baroque house like Beningbrough.

Investigations showed that so much had been altered in the Drawing Room – the panelling, the doorways and even the position of one of the fireplaces – that it would have been difficult to restore the room to its two constituent parts without great expense and considerable new work. The money was not available for this kind of operation. So a virtue was made of necessity: the room records an important social change in the use of the house.

In the stable block a substantially new interior has been fitted within the eighteenth-century exterior to take a shop, education room and other reception facilities. The restaurant between the stables and the house is the one new building at Beningbrough. Designed by Martin Stancliffe on the site of some dilapidated greenhouses, it makes much use of materials salvaged from elsewhere at Beningbrough. There were many abandoned buildings which required work before Beningbrough could reopen; the Victorian laundry, for example, has been restored, and the laundry courtyard cobbled. It is survivals such as these which have helped contribute to Beningbrough's success since its reopening in 1979.

In 2006 an entirely new display of the National Portrait Gallery's portraits on the first and second floors, designed by Casson Mann Ltd, was installed (described in more detail on p. 28).

Also in 2006 a lift was installed to give easier access to the upper floors. This was achieved without any major disturbance of historical fabric. The east courtyard has been flagged and recobbled to let people reach the lift entrance. At the same time, the historical appearance of window and door details was restored. The project also enabled us to reinstate the full enfilade on the first and second floors. From each end of the top floor, you can now look out of the windows, across the yards and gardens, and over an estate that has evolved since the 1550s. The spirit of the 2006 refurbishment of rooms, the reinterpretation of the portraits, and the installation of the lift was one of widening intellectual and physical access to visitors.

(Right) Conservation revealed that the panelling in the Drawing Room had been considerably re-arranged

List of pictures and sculpture

Works are listed clockwise from the entrance door into the room and may be subject to occasional alteration. All paintings are oil on canvas unless otherwise stated. Page numbers denote illustrations.

The Hall

John Churchill, 1st Duke of Marlborough (1650–1722) *with Colonel John Armstrong* (1674–1742)
By an unknown artist, *c.*1711–20 NPG 5318

William Russell, 1st Duke of Bedford (1613–1700)
By Sir Godfrey Kneller, *c.*1692 NPG 298

Queen Anne (1665–1714) *with her son, William, Duke of Gloucester* (1689–1700)
After Sir Godfrey Kneller, *c.*1694 NPG 325

Augusta, Princess of Wales (1719–72)
By Charles Philips, *c.*1736 NPG 2093

King George II (1683–1760)
Studio of Charles Jervas, *c.*1727 NPG 368

Prince George of Denmark (1653–1708)
By or after Michael Dahl, *c.*1705 NPG 4163

Frederick, Prince of Wales (1707–51) p. 6
By Philip Mercier, *c.*1735–6 NPG 2501

King George I (1660–1727)
By Sir Godfrey Kneller, 1716 NPG 5174

ON OVERMANTEL:

Pope Clement XIV (1705–74)
By Christopher Hewetson, 1771
Marble NT

The Great Staircase Hall

Sir John Perceval, 1st Earl of Egmont (1683–1748)
By Vincenzo Felici, 1707
Marble NPG 1956

Samuel Johnson (1709–84)
By Edward Hodges Baily, 1828, after a bust by Joseph Nollekens, 1777
Marble NPG 996

The North Front of Beningbrough Hall
By J. Bouttats and J. Chapman, 1751 NT

Sir Isaac Newton (1642–1727)
By Edward Hodges Baily, 1828, after a bust by Louis-François Roubiliac, 1751
Marble NPG 995

Sir Peter Warren (1703–52)
By Thomas Hudson, *c.*1751 NPG 5158

A Girl with a Mask
English School, *c.*1750–60 NT

James Cornewall (1698–1744)
By an unknown artist, 1730s NPG 5323

The Blue Bedroom

Charles Wilson, 1st Lord Nunburnholme (1833–1907)
British School, *c.*1880–90 NT

OVERMANTEL:

Lady Victoria Dawnay (d. 1922)
British School, 1890
Pastel
Gift of G. V. R. Grant NT

Florence Wellesley, Lady Nunburnholme (1853–1932)
By Edward Hughes, 1887 NT

Susannah Wilson (1865–1943)
By Ellis Roberts, 1890
Pastel NT

OVERDOOR:

Philip Dormer Stanhope, 4th Earl of Chesterfield (1694–1773)
By Allan Ramsay, 1765 NPG 533

The Closet

Group associated with the Moravian Church
Attributed to Johann Valentin Haidt, *c.*1752–4
NPG 1356

The Dressing Room

Charles Montagu, 1st Earl of Halifax (1661–1715)
By Sir Godfrey Kneller, *c.*1690–5 NPG 800

The Drawing Room (first half)

OVERDOOR:

Portrait of an Unknown Woman, formerly said to be Elizabeth Mackworth
British School, *c.*1700 NT

OVERMANTEL:

Portrait of an Unknown Woman, formerly said to be Mary Bourchier (1683–1746)
By Jonathan Richardson, *c.*1720 NT

John Bourchier the Younger (1710–59) p. 55
By John Vanderbank, 1732 NT

OVERDOOR:

Portrait of an Unknown Man, formerly said to be John Bourchier (1684–1736) p. 16
By Jonathan Richardson, *c.*1720 NT

The Drawing Room (second half)

John Christopher Pepusch (1667–1752)
By Thomas Hudson, *c.*1735 NPG 2063

OVERMANTEL:

Thomas Papillon (1623–1703)
By Sir Godfrey Kneller, 1698 NPG 5188

John Montagu, 4th Earl of Sandwich (1718–92) p. 16
By Joseph Highmore, 1740 NPG 1977

Alexander Pope (1688–1744) p. 17
Attributed to Charles Jervas, *c.*1713–15 NPG 112

OVERDOOR:

Portrait of an Unknown Woman, formerly said to be Judith English, Lady Dolben (*c.*1731–71)
British School, *c.*1750 NT

The Dining Room

All the Kit-Cat Club portraits in this room were painted by Sir Godfrey Kneller unless otherwise stated.

Charles Sackville, 6th Earl of Dorset (1643–1706)
*c.*1697 NPG 3204

Thomas Hopkins (d. 1720)
1715 NPG 3212

Charles Lennox, 1st Duke of Richmond and Lennox (1672–1723)
*c.*1703–10 NPG 3221

John Dormer (1669–1719)
*c.*1705–10 NPG 3203

Charles Mohun, 4th Baron Mohun (1675?–1712)
1707 NPG 3218

Richard Lumley, 2nd Earl of Scarborough (1688?–1740)
1717 NPG 3222

John Tidcomb (1642–1713)
*c.*1705–10 NPG 3229

Charles Howard, 3rd Earl of Carlisle (1669–1738)
*c.*1700–12 NPG 3197

Abraham Stanyan (*c.*1669–1732)
*c.*1710–11 NPG 3226

Algernon Capel, 2nd Earl of Essex (1670–1710)
1705 NPG 3207

William Walsh (1662–1708)
*c.*1708 NPG 3232

Charles Montagu, 1st Duke of Manchester (*c.*1662–1722)
*c.*1710–12 NPG 3216

John Vaughan, 3rd Earl of Carbery (1639–1713)
1700s NPG 3196

William Cavendish, 2nd Duke of Devonshire (1673–1729)
*c.*1710–16 NPG 3202

OVERMANTEL:

Jacob Tonson the younger (1682–1735) p. 19
*c.*1720 NPG 4091

Charles Dartiquenave (1664–1737)
After Sir Godfrey Kneller, 1702 NPG 3201

Charles Cornwallis, 4th Baron Cornwallis (1675–1722)
*c.*1705–15 NPG 3200

James Stanhope, 1st Earl Stanhope (1673–1721)
*c.*1705–10 NPG 3225

John Montagu, 2nd Duke of Montagu (1690–1749)
1709 NPG 3219

The State Bedchamber

OVERDOOR:

? Mary Bourchier (d. 1700)
By John Verelst, 1699 NT

William Congreve (1670–1729)
Studio of Sir Godfrey Kneller, *c.*1709 NPG 67

James Brydges, 1st Duke of Chandos (1674–1744)
By Herman van der Myn, 1725 or before NPG 530

OVERDOOR:

? Sir Barrington Bourchier (1672–1700)
By John Verelst, 1699 NT

John Locke (1632–1704)
By John Greenhill, *c.*1672–6 NPG 3912

John Dryden (1631–1700)
Attributed to James Maubert, *c.*1695 NPG 1133

The State Dressing Room

George Legge, 1st Baron Dartmouth (*c.*1647–91)
After John Riley, *c.*1690 — NPG 664

Also exhibited are engravings of William III and Mary II; and of the Kit-Cat Club by John Faber after Kneller; many of the original pictures are displayed in the Dining Room.

The Secondary Staircase Hall

King James II (1633–1701)
By an unknown artist, *c.*1690 — NPG 366

The Smoking Room

King William III (1650–1702)
By an unknown artist, *c.*1690 — NPG 1026

James Vernon (1646–1727)
By Sir Godfrey Kneller, 1677 — NPG 2963

The Seven Bishops Committed to the Tower in 1688
By an unknown artist, *c.*1688. — NPG 79

Samuel Pepys (1633–1703)
By John Closterman, 1690s — NPG 2100

Samuel Clarke (1675–1729)
By Jamé Verhych, 1719
Patinated lead — NPG 4838

The Saloon

John Churchill, 1st Duke of Marlborough (1650–1722)
Possibly by John Riley after John Closterman, after *c.*1690 — NPG 501

Unknown Youth
By John Closterman, *c.*1702–5 — NPG 1261

OVERDOOR:

Charles Talbot, 1st Duke of Shrewsbury (1660–1718)
After Sir Godfrey Kneller, *c.*1685 — NPG 1424

Abraham Tucker (1705–74)
By Enoch Seeman, 1739 — NPG 3942

George Frideric Handel (1685–1759)
Attributed to Balthasar Denner, 1726–8 — NPG 1976

OVERDOOR:

David Garrick (1717–79)
Studio of Johan Zoffany, 1763 — NPG 1167

Augustus Henry Fitzroy, 3rd Duke of Grafton (1735–1811)
By Pompeo Batoni, 1762 — NPG 4899

Catherine Macaulay (1731–91)
By Robert Edge Pine, *c.*1774 — NPG 1357

Philip Metcalfe (1733–1818)
By Pompeo Batoni, *c.*1766–7 — NPG 2001

Unknown Cardinal, formerly thought to be Henry Benedict Maria Clement Stuart, Cardinal York (1725–1807)
Circle of Anton Raphael Mengs, *c.*1750 — NPG 129

OVERDOOR:

Stag Hunting in Galtres Forest — p. 38
Manner of Jan Wyck — NT

The Children of John Taylor of Bifrons
By John Closterman, 1696? — NPG 5320

OVERMANTEL:

Philip Dormer Stanhope, 4th Earl of Chesterfield (1694–1773)
By George Knapton, *c.*1745 — NT

Maurice Ashley-Cooper (1675–1726) *and Anthony Ashley-Cooper, 3rd Earl of Shaftesbury* (1671–1713) — p. 24
By John Closterman, 1702 — NPG 5308

OVERDOOR:

Stag Hunting in Galtres Forest
Manner of Jan Wyck — NT

Lady Chesterfield's Room

Georgiana Cavendish, Duchess of Devonshire (1757–1806)
By Sir Joshua Reynolds, *c.*1761 — NPG 1041

OVERDOOR:

? Frances Bourchier
British School, *c.*1660–5 — NT

Margaret ('Peg') Woffington (1720?–60) — p. 4
By an unknown artist, *c.*1758 — NPG 650

OVERMANTEL:

Princess Louisa Maria Theresa Stuart (1692–1712)
Attributed to Alexis-Simon Belle, *c.*1704 — NPG 1658

OVERDOOR:

? Barrington Bourchier (1627–80)
British School, *c.*1650–5 — NT

Lady Chesterfield's Dressing Room

Prince Charles Edward Stuart (1720–88) p. 1
Studio of Antonio David, *c.*1729–32 NPG 434

Henry Benedict Maria Clement Stuart, Cardinal York (1725–1807)
Studio of Antonio David, *c.*1729–32 NPG 435

Joseph Gibbs (1699–1788)
By Thomas Gainsborough, *c.*1755 NPG 2179

Admiral Edward Vernon (1684–1757)
By Thomas Gainsborough, *c.*1753 NPG 881

Edward Boscawen (1711–61)
By Sir Joshua Reynolds, *c.*1755 NPG 5302

The East Landing

Grinling Gibbons (1648–1720)
After Sir Godfrey Kneller, after 1690 NPG 2925

Thomas Ripley (1682–1758)
By Joseph Highmore, 1746 NPG 5743

Constantine John Phipps, 2nd Baron Mulgrave (1744–92)
Attributed to Johan Zoffany, *c.*1774 NPG 1094

Sir Hector Munro (1725/6–1805/6)
By an unknown artist, 1785 NPG 1433

Henry Benedict Maria Clement Stuart, Cardinal York (1725–1807)
By Louis Gabriel Blanchet, 1738 NPG 5518

The Upper Corridor

The Emperor Vespasian (AD 9–79)
Italian School, *c.*1600
Bronze bust
On loan from Studley Royal NT

The Reading Room

Edwyn, 10th Earl of Chesterfield (1854–1933) p. 63
By F. E. Bertier, 1890 NT

Philip Dormer Stanhope, 4th Earl of Chesterfield (1694–1773)
By William Hoare of Bath NT

OVERMANTEL:

Elizabeth Davies (née Cattle)
By Orazio Manara, 1847 NT

Unknown Woman
By Sir John Steell, 1851
Marble NT

Enid, Countess of Chesterfield (1878–1957) p. 62
By Ellis Roberts, 1900 NT

IN PORCELAIN CABINET:

Unknown Man, called Richard Chesterfield
Continental School, *c.*1760–70
Miniature
Bequeathed to, and given by, the Dorset County Museum

Unknown Woman
? Anglo-Irish School, *c.*1750–60
Miniature
Bequeathed to, and given by, the Dorset County Museum

Family Matters

The Shudi Family p. 29
By Marcus Tuscher, *c.*1742 NPG 5776

The Talman Family
By Giuseppe Grisoni, *c.*1718–19 NPG 5781

Christopher Anstey (1724–1805) *with his Daughter* p. 28
By William Hoare, *c.*1776–8 NPG 3084

Portraits tell Stories

Ann (d. 1820) *and John Flaxman* (1755–1826)
By Henry Howard, *c.*1797
Oil on panel NPG 674, 675

Ann (d. 1820) *and John Flaxman* (1755–1826)
By John Flaxman, 1790–5
Plaster cast of medallions NPG 2487, 2488

Joshua (1716–74) *and Sarah Kirby* (d. 1775)
By Thomas Gainsborough, *c.*1751–2 NPG 1421

Thomas Jenkins (1722–98) *with his Niece Anna Maria Jenkins*
By Angelica Kauffmann, 1790 NPG 5044

James Wolfe (1727–59)
Attributed to J. S. C. Schaak, *c.*1767 NPG 48

James Wolfe (1727–59)
After Joseph Wilton, after 1760
Bronze NPG 2225

William Augustus, Duke of Cumberland (1721–65) p. 31
By Charles Jervas, *c.*1728 NPG 802

William Augustus, Duke of Cumberland (1721–65) p. 31
Studio of David Morier, *c.*1748–9 NPG 537

William Augustus, Duke of Cumberland (1721–65) p. 31
Studio of Sir Joshua Reynolds, *c.*1758–60 NPG 625

Thomas Day (1748–89) p. 30
By Joseph Wright of Derby, 1770 NPG 2490

Sir William Fawcett (1728–1804)
By Sir Joshua Reynolds, 1784–5 NPG 5515

Sir James Thornhill (1675/6–1734)
By Sir James Thornhill, 1710–25 NPG 5339

Robert Wood (1716/17–71)
By Allan Ramsay, 1755 NPG 4868

Charles Lennox, 3rd Duke of Richmond and Lennox (1735–1806)
By George Romney, 1775–7 NPG 4877

Getting the Picture

Susannah Maria Cibber (1714–66) p. 32
By Thomas Hudson, *c.*1749 NPG 4526

Matthew Prior (1664–1721)
By Thomas Hudson after Jonathan Richardson, *c.*1718 NPG 562

John Perceval, 2nd Earl of Egmont (1711–70)
By Thomas Hudson, 1759 NPG 2481

Dorothy, Viscountess Townshend (1686–1726)
Studio of Charles Jervas, *c.*1715 NPG 2506

Nathaniel Hone (1718–84)
By Nathaniel Hone, *c.*1760 NPG 177

Unknown Woman, formerly thought to be 'Peg' Woffington (1720?–60)
Attributed to Francis Hayman, *c.*1745 NPG 2177

Samuel Richardson (1686–1761)
By Joseph Highmore, 1750 NPG 1036

John Simpson (*c.*1738–*c.*1789)
By Angelica Kauffmann, *c.*1777 NPG 1485

Richard Boyle, 3rd Earl of Burlington and 4th Earl of Cork (1694–1753) *with his Sister, Lady Jane Boyle* (d. 1780)
After Sir Godfrey Kneller, *c.*1700
Oil on panel NPG 2495

John Carr (1723–1807)
By Sir William Beechey, 1791 NPG 4062

Lady Charlotte Finch (1725–1813)
By John Robinson, 1744 NPG 6205

William Pulteney, 1st Earl of Bath (1684–1764) p. 33
By Sir Joshua Reynolds, 1761 NPG 337

Richard Boyle, 2nd Viscount Shannon (1674–1740)
By Sir Godfrey Kneller, *c.*1710 NPG 3235

Turning Heads

John Michael Rysbrack (1694–1770) p. 34
Attributed to John Vanderbank, *c.*1728 NPG 1802

Isaac Ware (1704?–66)
Modern plaster copy after a marble bust by Louis François Roubiliac, *c.*1741 NPG D21387

Louis François Roubiliac (1702–62)
By Adrien Carpentiers, 1762 NPG 303

James Wyatt (1746–1813)
By John Charles Felix Rossi, *c.*1797
Bronze NPG 344

John Ligonier, 1st Earl Ligonier (1680–1770)
By Louis François Roubiliac, *c.*1761
Terracotta NPG 2013

Richard Colley Wellesley, Marquess Wellesley (1760–1842)
By John Bacon the Younger, *c.*1808
Marble NPG 992

Daniel Finch, 2nd Earl of Nottingham and 7th Earl of Winchilsea (1647–1730)
By Sir Godfrey Kneller, *c.*1720 NPG 3910

James Cook (1728–79) p. 35
By Lucien Le Vieux, 1790
Marble NPG 984

James Cook (1728–79)
Modern laser copy after Lucien Le Vieux, 1790
Marble NPG D21388

Spencer Perceval (1762–1812)
Studio of Joseph Nollekens, *c.*1812
Marble NPG 1657

Alexander Pope (1688–1744)
After Louis-François Roubiliac, after 1738
Terracotta NPG 2483

Warren Hastings (1732–1818)
By Thomas Banks, 1794 (1790)
Bronze NPG 209